Called to Marketplace Discipleship

Okoro Chima Okereke

Xulon
PRESS

Called to Marketplace Discipleship
by Okoro Chima Okereke

Printed in the United States of America

ISBN 9781619044623

Unless otherwise indicated, Bible quotations are taken from The New King James Version of the Bible.

www.xulonpress.com

Dedication

ȸ

I wish to dedicate this book in general to all who seek to glorify the Lord in their vocations and daily work as they face occupational and professional challenges. In particular, I dedicate it to three persons who have greatly influenced my life, they are: my parents and my wife. My father, Late Mazi Isaac Ukpo Okereke, to the best of my knowledge, tried to live a life of integrity and transparent honesty in his service to the public as a police officer and later as a customary court judge. To God be the glory that towards the end of his life, he became a Christian. My mother, Late Madam Mabel Ogbonneya Okereke, a hard working and determined lady, took her service of the Lord seriously throughout her life. My wife, Dr. Catherine Nnenna Chima-Okereke, a gifted and excellent medical practitioner, and an equally determined and hard working lady, who shows love and reverence for the Lord, in her private life and in the discharge of her professional duties.

Acknowledgements

℘

I wish to acknowledge that as I researched existing literature, I found a wealth of information on marketplace discipleship. Books and articles by Os Hillman, Rick Williams with Jared C. Crooks, etc., are in my assessment, excellent materials on the various aspects of the subject. It is not therefore surprising that I have quoted and adapted some materials from their works. I am thankful for the permission from Os Hillman to use them.

The contributions of my two pastors in the UK should go a long way to enhance the readability of the book. The first is Rev. Mostyn Roberts, pastor of the Welwyn Evangelical Church, Welwyn, Hertfordshire. Some years ago, I confided on him the burden I had to write this book. He tried to encourage me from time to time. When at last I produced my first manuscript, he reviewed it, and also reviewed the second manuscript. In each case, he made very helpful comments which I implemented. The second is my present pastor, Rev. Derek Simpson, pastor of Leominster Baptist Church, Leominster, Herefordshire. He read the first manuscript and made his criticism which I accommodated in the second manuscript. When he reviewed the second manuscript, he did it literally with a "sharp knife". He was thankfully thorough in his review and I had to discuss with him a few of his comments. Also, a retired pastor and a member of Leominster Baptist Church, Rev. Ken Morey, made useful contributions in his reviews.

From Nigeria, Professor (Mrs.) Onofeghara and Professor (Rev.) Onofegahara reviewed the book. My pastor in Nigeria, Rev. George Daniel-Oghenetega, pastor New Covenant Baptist Church, Port Harcourt, also made some comments. I should also thank others who attempted the review, including members of my immediate family. Catherine, my wife, showed interest. Uchechi, our youngest son, not only read it but also discussed his views with me and passed on the manuscript to some of his friends. Others were our two daughters; Onyinyechi and Chidinma, Onyekachi our second son; and Chibisi our first son who received the manuscript.

All these contributions have made the book a better product. However, if the reader finds it helpful, the glory should go to the Lord who initiated and guided the whole project. Finally, I bear responsibility for any defects on the book. Thank you.

O. Chima Okereke

Commendations

ᕫ

1) Concerning the book written by Dr O. Chima Okereke, I would be happy to commend it in the following terms:

"One word I would without hesitation use to describe my dear brother in the Lord 'Chima' Okereke, is integrity. As his pastor for several years in Welwyn, England, I knew him to be a man who wanted to apply God's Word in his personal life, in his family, in the life of the church in which he served faithfully as deacon for many years, and in the workplace. It is in relation to this last environment that Chima's concern to see the Christian light burn brightly has led to this book. It is rooted, as one would expect, in Scripture, but there is nothing merely theoretical about it. Chima speaks as a man who knows thoroughly the demanding world of work and as a Christian who seeks to serve his Lord there in life and word. He keenly desires all Christians to do the same. This book will challenge and encourage any believer to be the 'salt of the earth' in the workplace".

Mostyn Roberts,

Pastor, Welwyn Evangelical Church,

Hertfordshire, England, UK.

Phone: +441438 715372

My blog: http://harpfromthewillows.blogspot.com

2) From: Derek Simpson

Subject: Re Called to Marketplace Discipleship

I have been asked to provide a short piece for possible inclusion in comments about Dr. Okereke's book.

This is a timely book on an important topic. Dr. Okereke reminds us that it is the many witnesses living and telling the Gospel wherever God has placed them in their day to day lives that will get the message of Christ back into the culture. This is the answer to the question, 'How can they believe in the one of whom they have not heard?' that the apostle asked in his day and which has to be answered afresh in every generation.

Derek Simpson

Pastor,

Leominster Baptist Church, Herefordshire, United Kingdom.

3. From: George Daniel-Oghenetega

COMMENTS ON THE BOOK....."CALLED TO MARKETPLACE DISCIPLESHIP"

CALLED TO MARKETPLACE DISCIPLESHIP is a must read for all Christians. It is a timely reminder for Christians to have the correct perspective about their call in Christ, to live the Christian life in their daily work in the marketplace (profession, vocation, job, etc.) they find themselves. The sacred and secular works are both important to God. The average Christian should bring his faith into his vocation and shouldn't feel he is not in ministry until he goes into full-time sacred ministry. The author argues that for too long the dichotomy between the Clergy and the Laity has left the latter under 'lock and key', preventing them from being the ambassadors, ministers and witnesses they ought to be in their various market places for Christ. He also advocates a synergy between the clergy (pulpit) ministry and laity (marketplace) ministry. According to him, the clergy must recognize, equip and release the latter into their various spheres of influence if the Church is to bring about transformation in cities and nations. The various practical and relevant examples of ordinary people drawn from the Bible, past and contemporary history, who lived out their faith in their various professions and vocations to influence their cities and nations, sustain the reader's interest.

I wholeheartedly recommend this book to any Church that wants to fulfil the great commission.

COMMENTS BOUT THE AUTHOR: Dr. O. CHIMA OKEREKE.

I have known the author, Dr. O. Chima Okereke for quite some years. The close relationship that developed between us (he is a member of my Church in Nigeria), gave me insight into his personal and business life. He is a man of integrity, honour and honesty. He values people keeping their commitments.

I can confidently say he runs his business on biblical principles and sees it as his marketplace to be an effective witness for Christ. His life ties with the book he has written.
Rev. George Daniel-Oghenetega

Pastor,

New Covenant Baptist Church,

Port Harcourt, Nigeria

4) From: Kenneth Morey, B.A., Dip

CALLED TO MARKETPLACE DISCIPLESHIP by Dr O. Chima Okereke

The author, a Nigerian Christian businessman, has written a well researched and fully documented book, packed with both biblical and secular life stories illustrating his major premise that every Christian has "a calling to live for Him wherever He has placed us and shine the light of the gospel." He argues from an evangelical biblical perspective against a populist view dividing Christian ministry which falsely divides the secular from the spiritual. He demonstrates that "no role is less holy than another" and that the true believer not only lives a holy life for God in his workplace, but also sees it as his field of service for God. The book contains not only heart warming stories, but also soul searching questions and practical details of how change can be brought about. Dr. Okereke clearly sets out his motives for writing -in his own words, "One of the purposes of this book is to show that one can serve the Lord effectively and full time, even in one's secular work."

Kenneth Morey, B.A., Dip. Theol.

Friend of the author and former Missionary in Japan, Pastor in UK and Theology teacher in Eastern Europe & Africa – now retired.

Table of Contents

ℰ

1

Motivation to Write

ع

For some years before the 1970s, the Nigerian Fellowship of
Evangelical Students (NIFES) organized and supervised
Christian Union (CU) fellowship groups in different institutions of
higher learning in Nigeria. I became a Christian in 1970 through
the ministry of the Christian Union (CU) at the Federal School of
Science, Onikan, Lagos, Nigeria, at the end of the Nigerian Civil
War.

I was greatly helped to understand the implications and out-
working of the Christian faith as I listened to the talks given by
visiting speakers as arranged by our CU group with the help of
NIFES. One of the additional benefits that I personally derived
from the fellowship was access to very useful, helpful and relevant
Christian books which NIFES Travelling Secretaries brought to our
CU library and encouraged us to read. And as I did, I discovered
that they were very relevant to my needs as a young Christian. I
could find explanations to some of my problems, experiences and

the challenges that I faced. Titles like "Consistent Christianity" and "Keep Yourself Pure" are some of the titles of books that have been etched in my memory after I had read them. It was easy for me to include these and other Christian books into my library as I already had formed a personal habit of reading.

My reading of Christian literature was not confined to NIFES books as I also started reading books from such Christian book-shops as the Sudan Interior Mission (SIM) Bookshop, its name was later changed to Challenge Publications. Their bookshops had very rich stocks which were available at all their branches. It was heart warming to find them in some of the big cities that I visited such as Lagos, Enugu, Jos, Benin City, etc.

However, in the late seventies, it was with tears in my eyes that I saw the empty shelves that greeted me as I visited Challenge Publications Bookshop in Benin City, the capital city of the then Bendel State of Nigeria. I could not believe what I was seeing; all the helpful Christian books from Inter Varsity Press and International Fellowship of Evangelical Students (IFES), were all gone. On inquiry from the bookshop manager, I was informed that the then Nigerian Federal Government had banned the importation of Christian litera-ture. This was a fallout from the war.

It was driven home to me that if Christian books could no longer be imported, the time had come for Nigerian Christians to start pro-ducing their own books. It should become our responsibility to write books that will help build us up as Christians. Books that will help the young Christian understand and grapple successfully with the challenges of faith in contemporary society. Books that will present both to young and mature Christians our continuing responsibilities as people who have been called to live for the Lord as His ambassadors and shine the light of the Gospel of the Lord Jesus Christ wherever we are, irrespective of our societies.

It is the case that the ban on importation of foreign Christian literature was relaxed with time, yet, the urge for me to write remains. What is more, we Christians in developing countries have first-hand experience of our problems and failings. Therefore, the responsibility to get involved in solving such problem stares us on the face all the time.

Why "Called to Marketplace Discipleship"?

The title is an expression of the aims of this book which include the following:

1. To challenge us as Christians to work and live as disciples at our places of work such as in industry, businesses, academia, government, politics, etc.; that is in our marketplace.
2. To exhort us that as Christians, we are called to live as God's witnesses to make Him known in the world and also to be used as instruments for the edification and purification of our nations.
3. Our calling is to live for Him wherever He has placed us and shine the light of the gospel. Even as we belong to various vocations, our main purpose at our places of work should be to glorify

and honour the Lord. In calling us, He has made us His ambassadors to bear witness for Him among our colleagues in spite of global and national challenges that we may face.

4. To present the fact that whether we are workers in the marketplace or pastors at some churches, we are all called to full-time ministry. We are to serve the Lord and live for Him all the time wherever we are, whether at work or at church. Our behaviour and way of life should be consistent and pleasing to Him.

5. To inform us that we do not have to become pastors in order to serve the Lord. Therefore, the idea of abandoning a secular job for a spiritual job because that is supposed to show that we are seriously serving the Lord is not biblical. Therefore, our calling as Christians could be to full-time ministry in the clergy or full-time ministry in a secular job.

6. Our calling to any vocation is where the Lord has called us to serve Him. When we believe that the Lord has called us to the clergy, the objective is to use us for His glory and not for us to start our own church as an avenue for making money.

We Christians, for example in the developing world, are generally physically active and zealous in our worship services. In many of our countries, on Sunday mornings, most homes in cities, towns and villages, are emptied because almost everyone is at church. Also, in those towns and cities, most shops are not open for trading. Such is our zeal to go to church that close to ninety percent of the population in some of our towns and cities are busy, singing, dancing, or praying at church. In spite of this, however, our countries are among the most corrupt in the world. Outside the churches, the behaviours of most of us who go to church are similar if not the same as those of the non-church-goers. It is certainly true to say that if church-goers are free from the corruption, our countries will not be as bad as they are today. For it is written that "Righteousness exalts a nation but sin is a reproach to any people" Proverbs 14: 34. If therefore we Christians, who have the righteousness of Christ live a life of righteousness in the fear of God, sin will not have the dominion that it now has over us, over our businesses and over our nations.

As we read the Bible, we are faced with the truth that the Lord is not only interested in us as individuals but also interested in our nations. He wants us to live right to glorify His Name and walk with Him. He also wants to use us to reach our neighbours, contemporaries, compatriots, and others in our own world. We shall therefore explore how the Lord can use marketplace Christians to win their colleagues and fellow citizens. We shall consider how He will use us to heal our lands, villages, towns, and cities, indeed, our nations.

Objectives

Our objectives in this book are as follows:

1. To discuss the responsibilities of our callings as Christians and to explore and describe how we should live as marketplace Christians.

2. To realise that the Lord has called us as His instruments for evangelism, prayers, and other ministries that will make us shine the light of the Gospel in the marketplace in our nations. This calling should result in both temporal and eternal blessings for us as Christians, and for the healing of our nations as we walk with Him.

3. To describe some of our failures as Christians, and how we can be changed in order to become the people that the Lord intends us to be.

4. To highlight the fact that living for the Lord as His disciples requires that we are diligent at work. Laziness dishonours the Lord and damages our witness.

5. To recognise that the challenge to respond appropriately rests ultimately on each individual Christian. It is not quite a group response; just as we have been called as individuals, we are also accountable to Him also as individuals. There is therefore the call on each of us to submit to the Lord's control and respond as He directs and leads for His present and eternal glory.

6. To learn from examples of business persons given in the Bible.

7. To present the biographies of modern-day Christians of various professions so that we can learn valuable lessons from their lives.

8. To realise that even as we respond to the Lord as individuals, there could be the need for group actions as we work and pray for our nations.

2

Called to be a Christian: Called to Excellence, Called to be His Best

ॐ

"But you are a chosen generation, a royal priesthood, a holy nation, His own special people, that you may proclaim the praises of Him who has called you out of darkness into His marvellous light; who in time past were not a people but are now the people of God, who had not obtained mercy but now have obtained mercy". (1 Peter 2:9-10).

As children of God, we have been chosen by the Father and are called to represent Him as priests with the responsibility of becoming channels of blessings to mankind. Our merits as representatives are not based on our personal achievements but on what God has done for us, and continues to do through us, in Christ. We are a peculiar people, a people of the Lord, and should live such lives that reflect His holiness in our dealings in our communities. We are positively different, this difference has to be seen in our behaviours and contributions to the society and not just limited to what we say.

The difference will come as we seek to obey and live for the Lord. We shall get it wrong if we seek to live to please men but we should seek to please God. As we can see in Acts 4:19, the Apostles, Peter and John, told the Sanhedrin that they their obedience to God had to come first.

In Matthew 5:13-16, we have the following statements: "You are the salt of the earth: but if the salt has lost its flavour, how shall it be seasoned? It is then good for nothing but to be thrown out and trampled under foot by men.

You are the light of the world. A city that is set on an hill cannot be hidden. Nor do they light a lamp and put it under a basket, but on a lamp-stand, and it gives light to all who are in the house.

Let your light so shine before men, that they may see your good works, and glorify your Father in Heaven".

If we as Christians make no positive impacts on the world around us, we shall be failing in our profession as children of God. We should affect the world constructively just as salt seasoning brings out the best flavour of food. In addition, as salt is a preservative, we need to play our part in upholding and preserving or introducing Christian values, values that make for excellence, into our societies. One of the activities that could help the Christian make a positive impact at work and in the community is the excellence of our work, as we seek to work to please the Lord. "And whatever you do in word or deed, do all in the name of the Lord Jesus, giving thanks to God the Father through him" (Col 3:17). A case in point here is the life of

Daniel. "It pleased Darius to appoint 120 satraps to rule throughout the kingdom, with three administrators over them, one of whom was Daniel. Now Daniel so distinguished himself among the administrators and the satraps by his exceptional qualities that the king planned to set him over the whole kingdom. At this, the administrators and the satraps tried to find grounds for charges against Daniel in his conduct of government affairs, but they were unable to do so. They could find no corruption in him, because he was trustworthy and neither corrupt nor negligent." (Dan 6:1-4).

Daniel was an administrator in the Persian government of King Darius. Daniel was a model, God-fearing worker. He did his job so well that he was respected by his boss (the king) and became the source of jealousy of his colleagues. As Christians in the marketplace, we should find it instructive that when his colleagues conspired to find faults with him and his performance, they could not find anything against him. He was not corrupt. He did not betray the confidence reposed on him. He was diligent and not negligent of any of his responsibilities. Daniel was invariably an excellent worker. Excellence, in this usage, implies doing the best he could both in his performance and behaviour, all in the fear of the Lord.

It may be in order at this point to discuss a bit about the history of a businessman who was quite diligent in all he did. He was said to have been doing about three to four jobs at a time in order to redeem the time. He was Douglas Freeman.

Douglas Southall Freeman, Redeeming the Time [1]

"To my mind, there is no delight commensurate with that of a good long day's work", so Douglas Southall Freeman once wrote to his mother. He was born on May 16th, 1886 in Lynchburg, VA. His father was to him an excellent role model for business success, perseverance, and Christian faith. His father supported his family with excellent income from his farm but Douglas chose to go into business.

He was quite diligent at work. He earned his bachelor's degree from Richmond College (now the University of Richmond), and from John Hopkins University's graduate program in 1908 was awarded the Doctor of Philosophy in history degree, with subordinate applications in political science and political economy.

Just at the time that he was questioning his faith, he was invited to speak in a dingy, skid-row Richmond mission. In course of the message, former drunks, thieves and derelicts; their faces aglow with the glory of the new birth, stood up one by one and gave testimony to the life changing power of Christ's forgiveness. He was to confess that: "I saw men as sinful, perhaps, as I was who had been lifted out of themselves. If it works for them, it may work for me."

It was this experience that made him decide on his life work. He wrote: *"Every man must have his work, and that is mine — to labour earnestly, to labour honestly, and bring out something that may be worth men's while to read."* "I went to work for the Kingdom. I saw what the name of Jesus was doing with men, how this power was transforming their lives."

He had four full-time careers. He was an educator (teaching journalism at Columbia University), a historian and biographer, broadcaster (he had a daily commentary on Richmond radio stations for a number of years), and served as editor of *The Richmond News Leader*. He was a disciplined and hard worker who daily started his work at 2.20 AM and ended at 8.45 PM. His time management was legendary, he was quoted as saying: "scraps of time, "may seem so trivial they are not worth saving but the wise use of them may make all the difference between drudgery and happiness, between existence and a career."

He was quite devoted in his service to the Lord. For many years, he was active in the Second Baptist Church in Richmond where he was a member and a Sunday School teacher, just like his father before him. He had a small room in his home close to his study that included, an altar, complete with a cross, two candles, a kneeling bench, and a stained-glass window for prayer and meditation.

He was also active in local and national politics as an advisor to governors, senators, and even presidents. Woodrow Wilson made a habit of reading Freeman's editorials about the events of World War 1 every day. He also served as an advisor to Dwight Eisenhower and was reportedly instrumental in convincing Eisenhower to run for president.

Douglas Southall Freeman, biographer, historian, educator, businessman, and Christian leader, died on June 13, 1953 at 4:20 P.M. An epitaph for his life could be found in the words he wrote in 1948:

"I expect to die with a pen in my hand, with thanks to God on my lips for the opportunity of having led a life where I was permitted to work on the glorious yesterdays adorned by the noble figures whom I had the privilege of knowing."

Excellence means moral and ethical purity

Our nations are looking for the Daniels who will not only talk about avoiding corruption and living in holiness, but can be seen as not involved in corruption. They can be seen to be morally pure in their public and private lives.

Testimony: In 1971, some of us students lived a in a hostel in the Federal School of Science, Onikan, Lagos, Nigeria. Two students accused a Christian brother, who had travelled, of a dishonest action. Every Christian brother in the hostel, who heard the story, disagreed with the accusers. We insisted that their version of events could not have been correct. In his absence, we all defended him confidently and requested that we should all wait for his return to hear his account of the story. Two days after, he returned and when he was confronted, he narrated what happened. It became clear that he was completely innocent of their accusation. Our non-Christian colleagues were baffled that we defended him strongly even without hearing from him. What was more! His story on his return vindicated our confidence and trust in him.

It is the daily walk with the Lord, obedience to His word under the guidance of the Holy Spirit, that should make the believer able to live such a life of honesty. Transparent honesty is an essential virtue necessary for our light to shine as Christians in our own small corner of the world in the marketplace, especially in our corruption-ridden nations.

Transparent honesty and integrity are characteristics in short supply in our societies. Our lives and activities should demonstrate such qualities before our colleagues at work and school. The righteous and ethical living standard expected of Christians is underlined in Titus 2: 11-15: "For the grace of God that brings salvation has appeared to all men, teaching us that, denying ungodliness and worldly lusts, we should live soberly, righteously, and godly in the present age; looking for the blessed hope, and glorious appearing of our great God and Saviour Jesus Christ; who gave Himself for us, that he might redeem us from every lawless deed, and purify for Himself His own special people, zealous of good works. Speak these things , exhort, and rebuke with all authority. ....".

One of the easiest ways to discredit Christ in the marketplace, that is in our workplace, is for us to be lazy and do shoddy work. In order to gain the right kind of attention and reputation, our work should stand apart because we do it unto the Lord. "And whatever you do in word or deed, do it all in the name of the Lord Jesus, giving thanks to God the Father through Him" (Col 3:17).

Someone has suggested that doing quality work may not be the primary means of winning others to Christ, but habitually doing a poor job can disqualify us very quickly from ever having the opportunity to present Christ in a positive light. We need to go the extra mile when necessary so that when we do our work, we do it with excellence. We need to live with the realisation that God has called us to see our work as a calling from God. He wants to reveal His presence at our workplace where we spend a greater percentage of our time by shining as light for Him. Our doing quality and productive work should help the transformation of our economy and challenge our colleagues. Our calling goes beyond our work and includes our relationships to others — our wives, our children, our community and our nation. A Bible commentary on 1Peter 3:17 has it that "a living relationship with the Lord depends on right relationship with our neighbours". We must remember this to ensure that our "work calling" does not become elevated at the expense of the other important aspects of our life. This makes for the holistic approach to the gospel in which all aspects of our life are equally important.

Excellence means that Christians should be holy people, excellence presents a challenge

The challenge therefore is for us to become the type of people that the Lord wants us to become. We need church members, pastors, workers who will live and work as servants of the Lord Jesus Christ; we should live righteously and soberly whether we are pastors, workers in government, politicians, professionals, entrepreneurs, or businessmen, etc. We should recognise that we have been called by the Lord to live and serve Him wherever it has pleased Him to place us. We are His hands, feet, mouth, etc., to speak and work for Him in this world so that the light of the gospel of the Lord Jesus Christ can shine and bring more men to the knowledge of the truth.

We should have a consistent testimony, that should glorify the Lord, whether we work on sacred or secular jobs. In their book, "Your Work Matters To God", authors Doug Sherman and William Hendricks state the following with respect to holy versus unholy vocations. "The architect who designs buildings to the glory of God, who works with integrity, diligence, fairness, and excellence, who treats his wife with the love Christ has for the Church, who raises his children in Godly wisdom and instruction, who urges non-Christian co-workers and associates to heed the gospel message — in short, who acts as a responsible manager in the various arenas God has entrusted him — this man will receive eternal praise from God. That is what really matters in eternity. In short, God's interest is not simply that we do holy activities but that we become holy people. Not pious. Not sanctimonious. Not otherworldly. But pure, healthy, Christlike"[2].

Testimony: The writer knows a company in Port Harcourt, Nigeria, that professes to practise honesty and transparency in business. In October 2008, an engineer, from an oil service company, approached the consultants with a problem. He had been given a time limit within which he should have completed a 3-day hands-on course normally organised by the company. He informed them that he did not have the time to do the course but he was prepared to pay the full price of the course, N165,000.00, about $1,375.00, provided the company gave him the certificate as if he attended the course when he did not. He would then submit the certificate to his employers. He pleaded with them that his job was on the line but the consultants rejected the offer. They advised him to try to negotiate an extension of the deadline with his employers and that they would be prepared to organise for him to do the training within the time he would agree with his company. He left them dissatisfied. However, he returned early in 2009 and arranged to do the course. He under-went the 3-day training in February 2009. It was then that he made his payment and received his certificate. Christians need to take a stand for honesty even if it means apparent loss of income.

Called to be His Best - The Gospel Gets the Best out of the Individual.

The Bible does not leave us in any doubt that the Lord expects the best from His people. As already referred to earlier in this book, in Matthew Chapter 5, the Lord gives the beatitudes which sum-marise the standard of behaviour expected of believers. The chapter contains the highest ethical teachings on respect for the law, relation-ship with neighbours, teachings about lust, divorce, retaliation and even love for the enemy. It concludes in verse 48 with the words: "Therefore you shall be perfect, just as your Father in heaven is perfect". It is therefore inconceivable that anyone seriously walking with the Lord can be habitually ethically wanting. It is not that one has become morally perfect but it is that one has one's sight set on becoming perfect. It is also the case that one does not accept low moral standards as a way of life. This is clearly brought out in 1 John 1:6: "If we say that we have fellowship with him, and walk in darkness, we lie, and do not practise the truth." Therefore the excuse that everyone does it should not find any acceptance with the Christian because walking with the Lord and also deliberately continuing to practise corruption or any other form of sins are not compatible. It was this walk with the Lord that made the handsome and godly Joseph in the Old Testament (Genesis 39:9) to refuse and resist the advances of Potiphar's wife saying: "....There is no one greater in this house than I; neither has he kept back anything from me but you, because you are his wife. How then can I do this great wickedness, and sin against God?"

It was this walk with the Lord that made Daniel, (Daniel 6:1, 3-4), a model government administrator. It is the same God that we serve today. We are even in a more privileged position because we are in Christ, we can walk with Him every minute of our life, and also have free access to God. In John 15: 3, 5, the Lord says:

"Now ye are clean through the word which I have spoken unto ye. I am the vine, ye are the branches: He that abideth in me, and I in Him, the same bringeth forth much fruit: for without me ye can do nothing."

St. Paul underlines the adequacy of the Gospel to bring out the best in a person by stating in Romans 1: 16: "For I am not ashamed of the gospel of Christ, for it is the power of God to salvation for everyone who believes; for the Jew first, and also for the Greek."

The Gospel should bring the best out of us as we individually go into a personal relationship with the Lord Jesus Christ. Ephesians 2: 8-10: "For by grace are you saved through faith; and that not of yourselves: it is the gift of God; not of works, lest any man should boast. For we are his workmanship, created in Christ Jesus unto good works, which God hath before ordained that we should walk in them."

Therefore, God has provided through our individual personal walk with Him, a relationship that should bring the best out of each of us. Being pragmatic, we should ask ourselves whether we are living by the standard and ethical level that God has ordained for us. For, if we live in sin, God cannot use us, Isaiah 59: 1-2.

3

Vocation – An Outworking
of our Call

ॐ

Apostle Paul in Ephesians 4:1, writes: "I therefore, the prisoner of the Lord, beseech you to walk worthy of the calling with which you were called". The Lord has chosen us as His representatives in whatever vocation we are involved, using the gifts that He has given us to do our work and live our lives as worthy of His name. Therefore, the purpose of our calling requires that as followers of Christ we should live the whole of our lives in response to God's call.

We are first called into salvation, a holy, virtuous life of selflessness. This macro call of a Jesus-follower must limit our professional choices. We are not called into success or comfort or happiness. Doing one's best at work is expected in most vocations. The farmer, the soldier, the plumber, mason, the fashion model, etc., all use their abilities to do their best at their jobs.

In effect, the job each of us should do should be of such a nature that it can be seen as working for the Lord. This presupposes that it is constructive, ethical, a service to God and humanity. It should not present a hazard to mankind. Any job that will prevent us from living a holy life is not working for the Lord. For example, a job that makes products that will get people drunk with alcohol, or make money by selling illegal drugs, or through crimes and prostitution are not services to the Lord and should be avoided by any person who wishes to serve the Lord. The Christian should consider the following statements[3]:

- **If Christ is Lord over all of life, then he must be Lord over work, too.** In other words, whatever we do for work, we should do it "in the name of the Lord Jesus" (Colossians 3:17). This implies that our work should receive His approval and should be discharged in a manner that honours him.

- **All legitimate work matters to God.** God is a worker and has given man dominion over all He created (Psalm 8:6-8).

- **God designs people to carry out different kinds of work.** God fits us uniquely for certain kinds of tasks so that we can carry out his work in the world. That work includes not only spiritual tasks, but also extends to everyday fields of work.

- **God commends those doing good work.** "With good will doing service, as to the Lord, and not to men: knowing that whatever good anyone does, he will receive the same from the Lord, whether he is a slave or free." (Ephesians 6:7-8).

- **The Spirit empowers us to live and work with Christ-likeness.** We can expect the Spirit to enable us to use our God-given skills and abilities to bring glory to God, this has enormous implications for how we do our jobs.

- **God values our work even when the product has no eternal value.**

Will the work last? Will it really count for eternity? Our assumption is that God values work for eternity, but not work for the here and now. Ordinary jobs have only limited value, we think, because they meet only earthly needs. But this way of thinking overlooks several important truths:

- God's own creation is time-bound and temporary. Yet He values his work, declaring it to be "very good," good by its very nature (Genesis 1:31).
- God promises rewards to people in everyday jobs, based on their attitude and conduct (Ephesians 6:7-9).

- God cares about the everyday needs of people as well as their spiritual needs. To the extent that a job serves human needs, he values it because he values people.

God cares more about character and conduct than occupational status.

Paul's teaching in 1 Corinthians 12:28-31 is about various gifts, not vocations. At the time Paul wrote it, there were few if any "professional" clergy in the church. Paul himself was a tentmaker by occupation. Other church leaders practised a wide variety of professions and trades. God may assign rank among the spiritual gifts, but there's no indication that he looks at jobs that way.

■ Though our culture's hierarchy assumes sacred and secular distinctions and frequently assigns priority to the sacred (particularly among Christians), God does not. He values jobs, but his concern is for our character and our relationship with him.

Note: As acknowledged in the Reference Section, this material has been adapted from "Are Some Jobs More Important Than Others?" (2078) and "The Spirituality of Everyday Work" (2156) in The Word in Life Study Bible © 1993, 1996 by Thomas Nelson, Inc.

Our Vocation Requires a Holistic Approach

Our calling requires a holistic approach since every aspect of our life, in work, play, and prayer, should be done to the glory of the Lord. Sadly however, this response has often been distorted into a dichotomy that elevates the sacred at the expense of the secular. Out there in the real world, many Christians have been made to believe that there are two worlds, comprised of the sacred and secular, that should remain separated. Overtime, however, some Christians have challenged this error. As Os Hillman explains in his book: "Entrepreneurialism That Can Transform the 9 to 5 Window"[4], there is an unhelpful hierarchy that regards work as the bottom of the pile in Godly vocations. He writes: "We have an unwritten code that portrays a hierarchy of spiritual calling. It goes like this: The pastor holds the highest position, the missionary the next highest position, the church worker is the next highest, then comes the stay-at-home mum, then the secular worker and the CEO is the next to the last and then lowest of the lowest is – the lawyer"

It may be relevant, at this point, to review contributions of some Christian professionals in the marketplace in the service of the Lord and humanity. The Lord may use their lives to challenge us. Our objective should be to extract lessons and messages that could help us become effective as servants of the Lord Jesus Christ in our work and lives, especially in the marketplace.

1. John Beckett, a business owner and manager and writer, practises integrating his faith and his work so that his work can be meaningful and purposeful to glorify the Lord. He is a business leader who put his views across in his first book with the title: "Loving Monday: Succeeding in Business Without Selling Your Soul"[5]. The book is an account of how he has sought to integrate his faith and his work. It is said to be available in over twelve languages.

On this subject, he writes, "For years, I thought my involvement in business was a second class endeavour — necessary to put bread on the table, but somehow less noble than the more sacred pursuits, like being a minister or a missionary. The clear impression was that to truly serve God, one must leave business and go into 'full-time Christian service.' I have met countless other businesspeople who feel the same way."

In one of the chapters in "Loving Monday", he wrote this: "We usually think of calling in religious terms - such as calling to the ministry. But a calling to a vocation goes beyond the religious connotation. We can be called to the arts, athletics, to government services, or to business. If it is God's call, it is a legitimate and high calling. In other words, you can be an "ordained" plumber. People called to business have many opportunities unavailable to those who are specifically focused on ministry vocations".

Os Hillman, a Christian businessman and writer, who has written much on this subject. Some materials used in this book, including quotations, have been adapted from his writings. In each of the cases, appropriate reference has been made to acknowledge its source. An example is in reference [6].

A summary of his position is that "no role is less holy than another". Os Hillman, writes: "The often-held view by pastors toward business people was brought home to me one day when I received a letter from a pastor in response to an Internet devotional that I write for men and women in the workplace. This devotional is being distributed throughout the world and I have a surprisingly large number of pastors subscribed to it. One day I received a very simple note from a pastor that said, "How can a businessman have such wisdom?" This comment spoke volumes to me. Basically, he was implying that clergy were the only ones in tune with the spiritual matters of life, and businessmen and women are focused on the "secular" life. However, God has never said this. He is now helping many of us begin to understand our true calling as disciples of the Lord Jesus, but with different roles to fulfil in the body of Christ. And no role is less Holy than another".

Os Hillman writes: "When I received Christ in 1974, I was a golf professional. God gradually led me away from golf and into business. In 1980, I considered moving into "full-time" Christian work by attending a short-term Bible school to determine if I wanted to be a pastor. I served briefly as an assistant pastor only to have the position removed. God took me out of that because it was never His intention for me to be a pastor. It was more implied guilt than a genuine call of God that led me to consider "vocational ministry." I believed I might not have been giving my all to God if I wasn't full time in the work of the Lord. I have learned since then that work truly is worship to God: work and worship actually come from the same root Hebrew word, avodah. If you are in a secular job that doesn't violate scripture, your vocation is just as important to God as is a full-time missionary in India. God calls each of us to our vocation. It is in that vocation where He desires to use us for His kingdom".

The author has quoted the piece above from Os Hillman because it strengthens the point that we are called to serve the Lord full time in the positive and constructive vocation that He has placed us.

3. Professor Otto J. Helweg, Dean of the College of Engineering and Architecture at North Dakota State University, discussed in an interview how he had tried to find a balance between the sacred and secular[7]. His views in course of the interview are so relevant to this subject that they are summarised and attached to this information about him.

He says that he favours the division of work into the secular and sacred. He submits that there is a difference between writing a research proposal and sharing the gospel with a colleague. Without this approach, he suggests, "I fear some Christian professors may delude themselves into thinking they have no obligation to share their faith. They hide behind the assumption that closeting themselves in a lab is sufficient". In effect, he suggests that the dichotomy should be recognized so that it enables the Christian to attend to his responsibilities in the various areas, whether secular or sacred. In other words, the Christian should give adequate time to put in his best in the various challenges whether sacred or secular since we are stewards of our time, money, talents, etc.

It may be relevant to comment that the recognition of the dichotomy, as expressed by Otto, does not stem from the superiority or inferiority of the secular to the sacred as much as a recognition that seeks to elicit the best performance of Christians in attending to their responsibilities, whether secular or sacred. It is analogous to the Lord's command of "giving unto Caesar, that which is Caesar's."

Otto spoke of his failures and successes in achieving secular – spiritual balance as a Christian in academia. At this time of writing, he was the Dean of the College of Engineering and Architecture at North Dakota State University. He died on November 2, 2008. He demonstrated excellence in his academic pursuits as well as his ministry experience for the Lord. He received many awards such as in 1983, he was selected as the Ground Water Scientist of the Year for the U.S., the outstanding Civil Engineer in the state of Tennessee in 1994, the most outstanding engineer in the Mid South in 1995, and the Distinguished Research Award at The University of Memphis in 1995. He also received a commendation from the US Navy for saving them $2.5 million. He was an "eminent engineer" in Tau Beta Pi and a "doctor of service" for Blue Key. He received the 1997 Hoover Medal, which is the "Nobel Peace Prize" of the engineering societies in the United States. Past recipients have included Herbert Hoover, William Henry Harrison, Vannevar Bush, Dwight David Eisenhower, Sir Harold Hartley. The 1998 recipient was President Jimmy Carter.

The author of the initial article, published in Leadership U [7] wrote that they requested Dr. Helweg to talk with them about how he achieved balance between the demands of academic life and his spiritual obligations as a Christian professor.

The following is a summary of the views of Professor Otto Helweg on the Secular/Sacred Dichotomy as obtained from the interview:

1. Professor Helweg believes that there are two sets of issues on the balance of the secular and the sacred life of the Christian. They are theological(philosophical) and practical. On the first, he favours the division of work into the secular and sacred. He reasons that there is a difference between writing a research proposal and sharing the gospel with a colleague. He explains that without such distinction, some Christian professors may not give time to sharing their faith because they assume that their secular work in the lab or in research is sufficient.

2. He goes on to say that he thinks that the secular/sacred dichotomy was created by the Fall. He says that he does not think that before the Fall that there was secular. While the Fall did not create work, it cursed it by separating God's creation into a fallen world and the spiritual realm.

3. On a serious note, he says that he does not believe that the dichotomy should be eliminated. According to him, the tension will remain until the Lord returns.

4. On the practical issue, he submits that if we can categorize our work into the secular and sacred, then we should have the responsibility to balance the amount of time we spend on each.

5. He gives these definitions of secular and sacred:

Secular work is what is commonly known as one's profession or the work one gets paid for, whether it is as a professor or mechanic.

Sacred work is how one uses one's spiritual gifts and obligations, or "privileges," as a Christian, such as teaching the Bible, sharing one's faith, being an elder in one's church, etc.

He says that he believes that this distinction helps Christians who have personal vision and mission statements to manage their time better. He suggests that we need to remember that we are stewards of time just as well as stewards of our money and talents.

He supports his view with the following passages: Ephesians 5:14-17: "make the most of your time because the days are evil."

Proverbs 12:14: "the recompense of a man's hands will be rendered to him".

Proverbs 16:3 "Commit your works to the Lord, and your thoughts will be established."

Other passages show how Christians are enjoined to use their spiritual gifts, they are: 1 Corinthians 12-14 and also Romans 12 and Ephesians 4.

In effect, he believes that we are supposed to both use our time in our secular work as unto the Lord and also in the exercise of our spiritual gifts to the Lord. He submits that the distinctions are not made explicitly in the Bible but they are there implicitly.

6. He suggests that what we call secular work was created before the Fall. In Genesis 1:26-28, we have God commanding human-kind to rule over all the earth and subdue it. He says that he believes that God was saying, in effect, "Find out how I made this creation." I think this ought to form the basis for science and for Christian scientists who are fulfilling this command.

7. He explains that in Genesis 2:15, where the Lord placed Adam in the garden to "till" and "keep" it, both those words are even more obviously related to work. He thinks that it is very clear that in the act of creation God was at work. And so work is part of God's character, and Christians are called to work and to fulfil the purpose of their being.

8. He explains that Christian professors exhibit their excellence by being the best they can be. He continues that the Christian professor seems to be at a disadvantage in that he or she really has two careers: one in academia one in the church; I mean the larger body of Christ. He suggests that for most people this means that one's time to do research is limited because one also has to leave time for exercising one's spiritual gifts to build up the body of Christ.

9. He submits that: "on the other hand, the Christian has a distinct advantage that I fear is not utilized as much as it should

be and which many do not understand: the Christian has the Creator of the universe as a partner". He recommend that "Brother Lawrence's *Practice of the Presence of God* [Fleming H. Revell Co., 1999] should be required reading for every Christian because it encourages Christians to carry on a conversation with the Lord throughout the day. When professors are entering the classroom, preparing for experiments or writing a research proposal they should say, "Okay Lord, how are we going to solve this?" We need to constantly bring the Lord into these "secular" endeavors; and this actually creates an oxymoron because then we have a "sacred" secular task".

10. He gives a number of practical examples, testimonies from his life, and the following is one of them: "I remember working on my dissertation, ... and I was nearing the deadline. My wife and I sat down and prayed about it and "boom!" God just gave me the idea (the solution) while we were praying. That taught me a lesson. It doesn't make any sense to leave the Lord out of your problem-solving techniques in the lab".

11. He advises that professionals, whether academic or otherwise, should be careful to avoid the view that their work ("secular" work) serves the Lord as much as witnessing, for example. This unfortunately will encourage those who never witness to continue in their neglect of that task. He says that "Academia", like any other job which the professionals enjoy, "is a black hole; it will suck up every spare minute you have if you allow

it to do so. —the further problem is that academia, (like other profession) is almost addictive because for most of us our professional work is enjoyable and challenging".

He suggests "that in the spiritual battle, we are always led to believe that exercising our spiritual gifts is "hard work."" He says that because there are no "deadlines" (as such) "in our spiritual work" (as) we experience in academia (and other profession), "it is easy to replace our Christian responsibilities by those from academia (and other professions). He emphasises "And finally, we have the "prince of the power of the air" with his arsenal of weapons that keeps us from our sacred tasks".

12. He suggests that a person cannot escape the dichotomy of the secular and the sacred by enrolling in full-time Christian service. He says that he dislikes the phrase "full-time Christian service" because he thinks every Christian servant should be a full-time Christian servant. He says that "If I am doing the Lord's will throughout the day, I'm not a part-time Christian worker, I'm a full-time Christian worker". He concludes: "So while I think that some people are called to use their spiritual gifts full-time, others are not, and I don't think there should be a distinction."

13. He says that he has been able to incorporate his sacred life into his secular life by practising "the presence of God throughout the day and just carrying out a conversation with the Lord. It has almost become automatic for me to talk to Him if I'm going

between buildings, or find myself worshipping or singing to myself or something like that. Then there is the issue of making the conscious decision to bring Him into every problem and task that I have".

14. Finally, he suggests that Christians should "place both secular and sacred tasks under the Lordship of Jesus so that when they are making out a monthly, weekly or daily schedule, they can say, "Lord, we have thirty days—or 24 hours—how should we spend it?" We realize, of course, that God may want to modify our plans as we go along, but this prayer should give Christian professors great freedom, joy and confidence, so that when they are working, they should she feel God's pleasure.

4. R.G. LeTourneau

R.G. LeTourneau, a businessman from the United States in the early 1900s, wrestled with the secular versus full-time Christian work idea. He narrated the turning point in his understanding of how God desires to use business for His glory as follows: His pastor one day said to him, "You know, brother LeTourneau, God needs businessmen as well as preachers and missionaries." "Those were the words that guided my life ever since," said LeTourneau. "I repeat them in public at every opportunity because I have discovered that many men have the same mistaken idea I had of what it means to serve the Lord. My idea was if a man was going all out for God, he would have to be a preacher, or evangelist, or a missionary, or what we call a full-time Christian worker. I didn't realize that a layman could serve the Lord as well as a preacher. I left the parsonage in sort of a daze. If God needed businessmen, he could certainly find a lot better material than a dirt-mover with a lot of debts piled up in the garage business. But I said, 'All right, if that is what God wants me to be, I'll try to be His businessman'" [8].

An author has described him as "Moved by God to move men and mountains". A description of his performance by the author is as follows: "Few would disagree that the Allied invasion of Normandy in World War II on June 6, 1944 changed the course of history — the subsequent defeat of Hitler saved the free world from tyranny. The largest invasion army in history was accompanied by the largest array of machines and equipment in history, much of it built by R.G. LeTourneau" [8].

One of the statements attributed to him as he preached to different groups was: "If you're not serving the Lord, it proves you don't love Him; if you don't love Him, it proves you don't know him. Because to know Him is to love Him, and to love Him is to serve Him[8]". LeTourneau later became so wealthy and known for his generosity that he was giving 90% of his income to Christian causes.

5. Hoyt and Alfred Buck

Hoyt Buck was born in 1889, near Kansas City, Missouri, and he was the third of six children. While it was the case that he quit school after the fourth grade, he was a voracious reader who taught himself English, history, and mathematics, and even some Latin and Greek. He had the urge to travel and do things, such that in 1907, he travelled to Washington. In Tacoma, he did various small-time jobs such as selling insurance, working as a street-car conductor, etc. [9].

Hoyt was the pastor of an Assembly of God Church in Mountain Home, Idaho, when he had to respond to a call on a national emergency. After the debacle of Pearl Harbor, the US Government requested Americans to donate their fixed-blade knives to US Servicemen. Hoyt not only gave his knives but he also set up a blacksmith shop in the basement of his church and began manufacturing knives for the soldiers. As a result of the high quality of his knives because of his special tempering process, his knives were in high demand and became legendary among the soldiers.

At the end of the war, he moved to San Diego to work together in partnership with Al, his eldest son. They set up the first Buck manufacturing plant in a ten-by-twelve foot lean-to attached to Al's garage. This lasted just for one year as Hoyt died in 1948 of cancer.

Now Al, had to work with his wife and son, Charles, and in spite of the high quality of their products, the business was at the verge of bankruptcy in 1960[10]. It was then that the pastor of the family's church, Robert Wilson, intervened and convinced a quality control manager at Ryan Aeronautics, Howard Craig, to help. Craig and Al Buck, in fact, sat next to each other in the church choir. Moreover, Craig was knowledgeable about metals and part-owner of a small business that performed custom welding for airplane parts.

Following the advice of Pastor Wilson, the business was incorporated as Craig enlisted some of his business associates who joined Al to create Buck Knives, Incorporated on April 7, 1961. Without going into further detailed history, a number of points need to be highlighted for our education on the success of the Buck Knives Inc. They include the following:

1. They manufactured and sold top quality products.

2. They were God-fearing and are still God-fearing. It is interesting that it was Al's pastor, Wilson, that linked him up with Craig, and he in turn brought in other associates who worked with Al to make the enterprise a success.

From this humble beginning, the Buck Knives enterprise has grown to a multimillion-dollar corporation with a large manufacturing facility covering over four acres under one roof in El Cajon, California. The company continues to expand is now headed by the fourth generation of Bucks.

God the Senior Partner

The devotion to the Lord of the Buck Knives could be seen in one of the statements on their website: http://www.buckknives.com, written by Al Buck in 1976. This statement goes thus:

"If you are a new Buck knife owner, 'welcome aboard.' You *are now part of a very large family. Although we're talking about a few million people, we still like to think of each one of our users as a* member of the Buck Knives Family and take a personal interest in *the product that was bought. With normal use, you should never* have to buy another.

"Now that you are family, you might like to know a little more about our organization. The fantastic growth of Buck Knives, Incorporated was no accident. From the beginning, management determined to make God the Senior Partner. In a crisis, the problem was turned over to Him, and He hasn't failed to help us with the answer. Each product must reflect the integrity of management, including our Senior Partner. If sometimes we fail on our end, because we are human, we find it imperative to do our utmost to make it right. Of course, to us, besides being Senior Partner, He is our Heavenly Father also, and it's a great blessing to us to have this security in these troubled times. If any of you are troubled or perplexed and looking for answers, may we invite you to look to Him, for God loves you. John 3:16." By Al. Buck 1910 -1991

6. Dallas Willard

A Professor of Philosophy at University of Southern California, Los Angeles, a speaker and writer, says: "There is truly no division between sacred and secular except what we have created[11]. And that is why the division of the legitimate roles and functions of human life into the sacred and secular does incalculable damage to our individual lives and the cause of Christ. Holy people must stop going into 'church work' as their natural course of action and take up holy orders in farming, industry, law, education, banking, and journalism with the same zeal previously given to evangelism or to pastoral and missionary work."

Biography

He is a Professor in the School of Philosophy at the University of Southern California (USC) in Los Angeles[12]. He has taught at USC since 1965, where he was Director of the School of Philosophy from 1982-1985. He has also taught at the University of Wisconsin (Madison, 1960-1965), and has held visiting appointments at UCLA (1969) and the University of Colorado (1984).

His undergraduate studies were at William Jewell College, Tennessee Temple College (B.A., 1956, Psychology) and Baylor University (B.A., 1957, Philosophy and Religion); and his Graduate education was at Baylor University and the University of Wisconsin (Ph. D., 1964: Major in Philosophy, Minor in the History of Science).

He has written a number of philosophical publications mainly in the areas of epistemology, the philosophy of mind and of logic, and on the philosophy of Edmund Husserl, etc. He also lectures and publishes in religion.

He has served on the boards of the C.S. Lewis Foundation and Biola University, and is a member of numerous evaluation commit-tees for the Western Association of Schools and Colleges (accreditation). Dallas Albert Willard was born in Buffalo, Missouri, USA, September 4, 1935. He married Jane Lakes of Macon, Georgia, in 1955. They live with their children in Southern California, where Jane is a Marriage and Family Therapist.

Luncheon Remarks: Faculty Forum Luncheon Remarks by Dallas Willard at the C.S. Lewis Foundation Summer Conference, Univ. of San Diego, June 21, 2003

Below is presented a very useful luncheon remark by Professor Willard. Having read through it, it is considered quite educative and should be beneficial to readers. We have therefore reproduced its highlights. It was during the C.S. Lewis Foundation's Western Regional Conference at the University of San Diego on June 19-22, 2003, that Dr. Willard was asked to speak at a Faculty Forum luncheon on the topic, "My Journey To and Beyond Tenure in a Secular University."

The relevant part of his speech that concerns the Christian attitude to work, secular or spiritual is as follows:

1. He says : "My strategy was this – do really good work. Do work that you would think God had to help you with to get you there, and then do some more. Just stay at it. That's the only strategy I've had is to work in that way".

2 He assumes that the Christian should be in a good field. He says: "My view is that, if you are in a good field, you must work on the

things that are really central and essential to that field. And you ought to believe that God will enable you to do work in that field that will be a benefit and challenge to everyone".

3. He exhorts us to do really a good work, indeed more than our best. He writes: "— what we as Christians want to do — we want to get to the point where people scattered around the academic world are worried about what we are doing. They sit up at night and think about us. They get on the internet, and they chase our work down. I really challenge you to believe that about yourself, whatever your area of work is. Not because you are so good, but because God is so great".

4. He commits his academic work to the Lord: "I try to teach classes well. I pray for my students. I pray as I set up the course schedule and the outline. I pray for them when they come in to interview. They don't know I'm praying most of the time, but I pray for them, and I pray for the class. I say, "Lord, let this be a class that will really help these students in their work, in their field, in their self-confidence.""

5. He says that he is not there to be a witness but to do the best work with the help of the Lord and as he does this he becomes a witness. In other words, he does not go with bible text to witness to his students rather he goes to do the work that he can possibly do and the Lord uses that to witness. He writes: "I'm not there to be a witness. I'm there to do a good job as a teacher and writer. I will be a witness. I can't help that. The only question is, "What

am I going to witness to?" And I take a lot of comfort from Jesus' statement that you cannot hide a city that is set on a hill. So I don't have to think about it. I have to try to do real good work; and that's my business – to do real good work. I wouldn't say it's the best in the world or anything like that, others can make judgements, but my intention is to do the best work possible. And by that I don't mean within my human limitations; I also mean God helping me. I'm going to put my human limitations on the line, but my expectation is not from them. I expect to see something happen that I could not possibly do. And I would do that if I were preaching or witnessing on the streets, or doing whatever wherever".

4

God Ordained Secular Work

ↄ

We read in Genesis 1:28: "Then God blessed them (man and woman) and God said unto them, "Be fruitful, and multiply; fill the earth, and subdue it; and have dominion over the fish of the sea, over the birds of the air, and over every living thing that moves on the earth". In this passage , we see the Lord God giving man the responsibility to work on the earth and have dominion over every living thing. This was even before the fall. It is the case that before and after the fall, God had ordained work for man to do. "And w*hatever you do, do it heartily, as to the Lord, and not to men, knowing that from the Lord you will receive the reward of the inheritance: for you serve the Lord Christ.*" Colossians 3: 23-24.

The first man filled with the Spirit of God was ordained for work. As we go through the passage, we shall highlight verses on work that the LORD spoke to Moses, Exodus:31: 1-11:

- "See, I have called by name Bezalel the son of Uri, the son of Hur, of the tribe of Judah.

- And I have filled him with the Spirit of God, in wisdom, in understanding, in knowledge, and in all *manner* of workmanship,
- To design artistic works, to work in gold, in silver, in bronze,
- In cutting jewels for setting, in carving wood, and to work in all *manner* of workmanship.
- And I, indeed I, have appointed with him Aholiab the son of Ahisamach, of the tribe of Dan; and I have put wisdom in the hearts of all who are gifted artisans, that they may make all that I have commanded you:
- The tabernacle of meeting, the ark of the Testimony and the mercy seat that is on it, and all the furniture of the tabernacle—
- The table and its utensils, the pure gold lampstand with all its utensils, the altar of incense,
- The altar of burnt offering with all its utensils, and the laver and its base—
- The garments of ministry, the holy garments for Aaron the priest and the garments of his sons, to minister as priests,
- And the anointing oil and sweet incense for the holy *place*.
- According to all that I have commanded you they shall do."
- **Lastly, God commanded the use of workmen to build the Temple. The passage continues :** "Moreover *there are* workmen with you in abundance:

- Woodsmen and stonecutters, and all types of skilful men for every kind of work. Of gold and silver and bronze and iron *there is* no limit.

- Arise and begin working, and the LORD be with you." 1 Chron 22:15-16 (NKJV)

God the Creator – A Worker

When God created the earth, He demonstrated to us, humans, that He believed in work. He was above all else, the Master Creator. He was an artist, designer, strategic planner, organizer, project developer, assessor, zoologist, biologist, chemist, linguist, programmer, materials specialist, engineer, and waste management technician, all rolled into one. This work did not end when He created man, but was only the beginning in His continued care for mankind.

Our Work is our Calling

In his article, "Assigned to Design" [13], Andrew Patrick, a Christian and an architect in the UK, discusses career and vocation. He writes: "'Does God care which route I follow?' 'Is this God's plan for me?' asks a fresh Town Planner student about to embark on her career. 'Is he concerned about which career I follow?' 'Where do I go from here?' ponders a mature Christian architect as he reviews his work history in mid-life".

He continues: "I believe we need to answer these questions because God is looking for men and women who want to obey and serve Him in *every* aspect of their lives. He wants to use our daily living to convert heathen nations and restore nations that once belonged to Him but are drifting away. We need to answer these questions because the world is looking for Christians who actually live what we say, on the drawing board, at meetings, in the plans we produce, and on site. How else can the world see that Jesus is alive?" [13]

Diversity of Gifts, Callings, Vocations, and Work with God

The Lord has created us as different individuals with diversity of gifts and talents. This diversity enables us to be equipped for different vocations. As a result, a job that one person may not find appealing may be attractive to another person. In spite of all the various talents, it is as we obey Him in the discharge of our daily tasks in our vocations that He brings the best out of us.

Obedience is the Primary Requirement

The Bible greatly emphasises obedience to the Lord irrespective of our vocations. Indeed, a book can be written on the subject because it is the number one requirement that any individual working with God has to meet. If any individual is not prepared to obey the Lord, then he cannot walk with Him. There are no two ways about this non-negotiable condition of discipleship. The emphasis on obedience is underscored in the wonderful, indeed miraculous, catch of fish by seasoned fishermen who had toiled all night without a catch.

However, when the Lord appeared and directed them to where to throw their net, reluctant as they were, and probably intrusive as they might have considered the instruction, they obeyed the Master. We know the rest of the story; how they caught "a great number of fish, and their net was breaking." (Luke 5: 3-10). It is equally relevant that they had obeyed the Lord before then by providing their boat as the lectern for His use as "He sat down and taught the multitudes" (Luke 5: 1-3).

We know that in our everyday walk with the Lord and in our obedience to Him, we do not record what we may consider miraculous catches everyday. However, the fact that we have the assurance that we are working and walking according to His purposes should be rewarding.

Oswald Chambers provides some valuable insight into the call of God. He writes: "The call of God is a call into comradeship with the Lord Himself for His own purposes, and the test of faith is to believe that God knows what He is about. The call of God only becomes clear as we obey, never as we weigh the pros and cons and try to reason it out. The call is God's idea, not our idea; and only on looking back over the path of obedience do we realize what God's idea has been all along, for God sanctifies memory"[14]. Briefly put, it is as we work and walk with the Lord in faith and obedience that the Lord uses us to achieve His purposes and to work out our calling in Him and in the world. This is clearly demonstrated in the life of Joseph. He stuck to the path of obedience and suffering even when he was falsely accused, denied justice and imprisoned, he did not give up on his walk with the Lord. God's plan for his life was consummated as he was taken from prison to the second highest position. It is quite easy to overlook the fact that he had earlier spent years of training in obedience and faithfulness to the Lord, as he served in Potiphar's house and in prison.

Our Background and Interest are a Launch Pad for our Vocation and Calling

The Lord takes us through various experiences and backgrounds in our individual lives to allow us to develop specific skills and talents for His purposes. God gives each of us a work to do that flows from our relationship with Him, our Heavenly Father, through the Lord Jesus Christ. That work is designed to meet the needs of mankind. This is why God gives each person unique skills and abilities.

Yes, the Lord uses our background and the early training, like David's, to prepare us for future tasks that God will use for His purposes in our lives. He also uses our talents and the abilities which He has enabled us to acquire for His greater glory. For some of us, we use these talents to provide valuable services to our employers, or we use them in business as entrepreneurs, all in obedience to the Lord and for His glory. We can find comfort in the knowledge that there is no higher calling than to be where God calls us. Regardless of whether it is in "full-time" Christian mission work, or working at the local shop, in a political office, government department, etc.

"And let the beauty of the Lord our God be upon us, and establish the work of our hands for us—yes, establish the work of our hands" (Psalm 90:17). In other words, as we are doing the work God has called us to perform, the Lord in His favour is establishing the work of our hands as a spiritual service unto Him. One of the historical examples of the Lord using our background to equip us for our calling as a service to humanity and for His glory is William Wilberforce.

William Wilberforce was an international transformer in his days. Although he did not cause a city transformation movement, he worked with his colleagues to lead world-changing initiatives that changed society. The most notable was the abolition of slavery in England after 30 years of work.

William Wilberforce was known as the George Washington of humanity in England. He was responsible for eliminating slavery in England after 50 years of working towards achieving it. This was realised through world-changing initiatives that he started with his colleagues which changed England and the world.

He was born on 24 August 1759 in Hull, the son of a wealthy merchant and studied at Cambridge University [15]. In 1780, Wilberforce became member of parliament for Hull, later representing Yorkshire. His loose lifestyle changed completely when he became an evangelical Christian, and in 1784 joined a leading group known as the Clapham Sect. His Christian faith prompted him to become interested in social reform, particularly the improvement of factory conditions in Britain.

He and his colleagues started campaigning for an end to the trade in which British ships were carrying black slaves from Africa, in terrible conditions, to the West Indies as goods to be bought and sold. Wilberforce was persuaded to lobby for the abolition of the slave trade and for 18 years he regularly introduced anti-slavery motions in parliament. The campaign was supported by many members of the Clapham Sect and other abolitionists who raised public awareness of their cause with pamphlets, books, rallies and petitions. In 1807, slave trade was finally abolished, but this did not free those who were already slaves. It was not until 1833 that an act was passed giving freedom to all slaves in the British empire.

His passion was politics and government laws. When he became a Christian, he immediately proclaimed that he wanted to pursue more noble and spiritual endeavours. By this, he meant to become a clergy. His spiritual mentor was John Newton, who wrote the very popular hymn, *Amazing Grace*. He dissuaded him from thinking that serving as a cleric was more important than his call to work as a politician and encouraged him to stay in politics. Newton could see that God had placed this calling upon his life. With the benefit of hindsight, we cannot thank the Lord enough for that wise counsel that kept William in politics. For his activities resulted in so much good for mankind. His story underscores the point that the Lord could use our gifts, talents, and background, whether secular or sacred, for

His glory and purposes and for the benefit of humanity as we walk with Him. Yes, whether our calling is secular or sacred, the Lord will use it to His glory if we are where He wants us. For the story of William Wilberforce cannot be complete without the part played by John Newton who the Lord used to advise him to stay on in politics. John was a slave dealer who made many voyages from Liverpool to Africa and the West Indies on slave trading. When he became too ill to continue and took up a job with the customs in Liverpool and later became an evangelical Christian. He was ordained and became a curate, an assistant to the vicar in Olney, north west of London. In 1788, as a vicar of St. Mary's Woolnoth, London, he published a pamphlet entitled "Thoughts Upon the African Slave Trade". In this pamphlet, he wrote from first hand experience as slave dealer for thirty years on the evils of the trade. The pamphlet sold out on its first edition and he sent a copy of the second edition to every MP. He also testified at parliamentary hearings. We therefore have much cause to thank the Lord for using the experience of seasoned slave dealer to work for the abolition of slave trader when he became a clergy.

5

Our Primary Call

ॐ

We need to remind ourselves that each of us is called to a personal relationship with God through Jesus Christ, first and foremost. We are his "workmanship created in Christ Jesus for good works.."(Eph. 2: 10). Whatever career job we do, we should see it as our God-given call, whether serving as a local pastor, or on the mission field, or in a government office, or in politics, or in trading, or in such professions as the clergy, medical, teaching, engineering, legal, etc. The Lord has created each person in His image for His purpose in this world to reflect His glory in ALL aspects of life. He has made us with various backgrounds to fit into assignments that He has for us.

Shining the Gospel Light: The Christian at Work and a Framework for Living

So far, we have touched on the so-called split between the sacred and secular in the life of the Christian. In view of which, some

Christians tend to live in two separate worlds; the sacred world which is expressed in the family and church and the secular world lived in the public and workplace where religion is not generally expressed. In the public and at work, many Christians mostly practise their faith by being ethical on the job, that is transparent living such that there is no lying or cheating. Beyond this, the objective of the work is to "put food on the table" with a regular salary cheque, climbing the career ladder, and probably excelling as a professional. Workers spend greater parts of their career lives at work. In some cases, children hardly see their parents because they leave very early to work, probably when the children are still asleep, and return very late when the children have gone to bed. This writer has heard some parents comment that when they met with their children during the weekends, they complained that they had not seen them for some time. In addition, as noted earlier, at work, some people's faith is "under lock and key", not to be expressed freely. This invariably leads to the dilemma for Christians of how they practise their faith and how they can impact it on society and on work colleagues and systems in the marketplace.

As one reads about the contributions of many Christian writers on marketplace discipleship, one may see the need to suggest that Christians require individually to find or prepare prayerfully a practical work and behavioural set of guidelines that could constitute a framework that they can use to help them give their best in both sacred and secular responsibilities. A framework that enables them to do their public work with honesty, integrity, and dedication as unto the Lord in demonstration of their calling. At the same time, a framework that prods them to live in the realisation that their ability to serve effectively in their vocations is dependent on their relationship with the Lord, a relationship that should reflect their daily walk with the Lord. A framework that enables them also to live daily in light of their Christian responsibilities of daily personal devotion and contributions and service to their local church, fellowship and families. A framework that should help them analyse the temptations in their work environment and prepare them pro-actively to address successfully the possible technical pressures and ethical minefields in their marketplace. Such a framework should be founded on the word of God, the Bible through the guidance of the Holy Spirit. It should be correct to submit that biblical principles hold good in every human endeavour including all the various vocations.

Christians at Work in the Frontline for the Gospel – in the Marketplace

Marketplace Christians are those at work in business, industry, politics, factory work, and so on. These are the Church's frontline troops in its engagement with the world, so wrote Lesslie Newbigin[16]. He continues: "Imagine how our churches would be transformed if we truly regarded laypeople as frontline troops in spiritual warfare. Are we taking seriously our duty to support them in their warfare?" Newbigin asked: "Have we ever done anything seriously to strengthen their Christian witness, to help them in facing the very difficult, ethical problems which they have to meet every day, to give them the assurance that the whole fellowship is behind them in their daily spiritual warfare? The church should be nothing less than a training ground for sending out laypeople who are equipped to speak the gospel to the world".

"In a sense, Christians need to learn how to be bilingual, translating the perspective of the gospel into language understood by our culture. On one hand, we all learn to use the language of the world: As we go through the public education system, we become trained to use the language and ways of the world without the hypothesis of God,"[17] as Newbigin puts it. But then, for about an hour or two a week, we use the language of the Bible. He suggests that we should live like immigrants, even as the Bible puts it, we are in the world but "not of the world" John 17:16. As Christians, we are not called to live only like immigrants, simply preserving a few customs and phrases from the old country, the word of God; instead, we are to live and work like missionaries, actively translating the language of faith into the language of the culture around us. According to Newbigin, the uncomfortable truth is that we do not seem to be doing very well as most Christians do not know how to express their faith in their world environments such as at their places of work and relationships outside their families. Like immigrants, who have difficulty adapting to their new homes, we have not yet mastered how to express our faith in public, we are self-conscious. In private, that is in our churches and homes, we express our faith to one another, but in public, generally we do not have the confidence to do so.

Lesslie Newbigin goes ahead to discuss how some nations relate their faith to their whole lives. For example, for the Indian Christians, he explains that their mentality is that religion permeates all of life. He continues that in most human cultures, religion is not a separate activity set apart from the rest of life. In these cultures, what we call religion is a whole world-view, a way of understanding the whole of human experience.

A brief biography of Lesslie Newbigin 1909 - 1998

Much of this information has been taken from a material written by Maynard[18]. **James Edward Lesslie Newbigin** was born in Newcastle upon Tyne, England, on December 8, 1909. He schooled in Leighton Park, the Quaker public boarding school in Reading, Berkshire and Queen's College, Cambridge. He was said to have started at the school in 1928 as an agnostic, but following the witness of an older student to him in his first year, "he slowly moved past his doubt and (moved) into the Christian faith"[18]. As he slept one night at the age of 19 in a Quaker service centre in South Wales, he saw a vision that helped change his life. He saw a "cross touching, as it were, heaven and earth. The cross embraced the whole world and the whole of life"[18].

Newbigin has been described in general as "Highly disciplined and mastered the basics of whatever he studied, and was thoroughly prepared for each assignment. He showed a gift of and pursuit for excellence in everything he undertook. He was a linguist, administrator, ecclesiastic, theologian, missiologist, preacher, pastor, epistemologist, author, limerick writer, rock climber and doughty fighter, but all his talents were used in the service of his missionary evangelistic vocation"[18].

In July,1936, he was ordained by the Presbytery of Edinburgh to work as a Church of Scotland missionary at the Madras Mission and sailed to India in September 1936. He was one of the architects of the Church of South India and became one of its first bishops when he was appointed in 1947. He retired in 1974. On his return to the UK he found it a changed place. It was no longer the home he left for India. However, he settled in Birmingham and became a lecturer at the Selly Oak Colleges for five years, before becoming the pastor of a United Reformed Church (URC), and later the Moderator of the URC for 1978-79. He was a prolific writer and "established himself as one of the most respected and significant theologians of the Twentieth Century."

Until his death on January 30 1998, he was said to have proclaimed "the gospel as "public truth", in the public domain because it is not just religiously true but true all the way down." He continued to explore ceaselessly "for a missionary encounter with our brilliant but pagan western culture."

The author has been challenged for including the biography of Leslie Newbigin, a clergy, in this book which should contain biographies of secular men. The reason one would proffer is that Newbigin was not just a clergy in that sense of the word, where one was purely concerned with one's church and members. No, he was a clergy who saw the whole world as his mission field and the church, a training ground for preparing workers, professionals to live out their faith in their everyday vocations to the glory of the Lord.

A Company of Prophetic Apostolic Business People and Workplace Ministry

Thus far in this book, we have made the point that Christians should glorify the Lord in their public lives and vocations by allowing themselves to be led by the Holy Spirit in applying biblical principles in their secular activities and jobs. Our focus has been on Christians as individuals because we work as individuals in our various jobs. It becomes exciting when we read of Christian organisations whose ministry it is to prepare Christians to perform their secular and professional jobs as service to the Lord. One of such organisations is the Christian International Business Network (CIBN), a division of Christian International. It is a church-based ministry with a goal of raising up a "company of prophetic apostolic business people," according to the ministry's vision statement. CIBN has developed networks for church-based workplace ministries in the United States and some other countries.

Another such group is the California-based "His Church at Work" ministry. It tries to equip the local church to focus on faith at work issues. Doug Sherman, author of *Your Work Matters to God*, cautions that the local church has been slow to embrace this message. "Our surveys reveal that 90 to 97 percent of Christians have never been trained to apply biblical faith to their work life," says Sherman. However, Doug Spada's California-based *His Church at Work* ministry is one of the pioneering efforts to equip the local church to focus on faith at work issues. Doug Spada, a former nuclear submarine engineer and entrepreneur is the founder and President. He carries out this ministry by creating the infrastructure for a sustainable work-life ministry. His ultimate vision is that churches will send out members to minister in the workplace, just as missionaries are sent out to foreign lands[19].

"We help people launch full-blown ministries within their church," Spada explains. "This isn't, 'Hey, let's meet for breakfast.' This is more of an embedded ministry which makes it part of the DNA of the local church." Beyond that vision, Spada says there's a broader reason for the local church to be creating work-life ministries. "Spiritual renewal movements, particularly in Western culture, are almost always birthed and driven by all segments of a working society, not just the leaders."

Karen Jones, director of workplace ministry at Southeast Christian Church in Louisville, Kentucky, agrees. "I believe it is a move of God. I believe it's cutting edge — the next mission field." Southeast Christian Church launched its workplace ministry two years ago based on Spada's model, and Jones says her initial goal is to involve at least half of the church's 20,000 members. "Statistics say that each person has a sphere of influence of about 25," she comments. "So we could be influencing 250,000 people a week very quickly if people understood that their workplace was a mission field." The impact in the community could be tremendous.

In his book ,"The Spirit of the Disciplines: Understanding How God Changes Lives", as highlighted earlier, Dallas Willard suggests that Christians should do their secular work to the glory of God with the same zeal originally given to evangelism and missions. The message is getting through as the Faith at Work movement sweeps across the land, and has the potential to lead to genuine revival across the culture.

A brief biography of Doug Spada and the WorkLife Incorporated

Spada was a Navy veteran, a successful entrepreneur in Southern California who started Utili-Tech, Inc., an energy and utility services firm that worked with companies like ARCO, Texaco and Exxon. In spite of his business success, Spada said he became "spiritually burdened for people's work lives" and prayed to God for guidance in using his talents in ministry [19].

"People are happy in the pews letting 'professionals' do this," said Doug Spada, a Navy veteran in nuclear engineering who started HisChurchatWork.org in 2002 at Journey Community Church in

San Diego and later based in Alpharetta, Ga. "We need to shift from going to church to being the church."

Journey Community Church allowed Spada to start a pioneering church-based worklife ministry based solely on biblical principles drawn from such passages as Ephesians 4:11-12. From that, HisChurchatWork.org was formed.

"Why did I do this? It was me being obedient," Spada said. "I was privately discouraged, disconnected, disillusioned in the area of my greatest influence.

"Churches think programmatically. They spend millions of dollars on programs and then people get saved when the pastor preaches. Pastor says God called him to the ministry. What about the people in the pew? What are they called to do? We help churches build bridges where walls and gaps existed. Our mission is to make sure every church leader wrestles with this. We teach churches how to sustain efforts to disciple the scattered church, whether it's the bus driver, teacher, engineer or stay-at-home mom. We define work as what God defines it, which is the essence of work, not just a place you go"[19].

Spada has been working with churches to provide training in worklife ministry through a program called Worklife University, encompassing 30 modules of training. He provides support staff and also links and resources for the church's website in order to "train the trainers" and help the church fulfil its greatest impact at the marketplace during the work week.

"They then train the layperson to lead the ministry," Spada said. "It's important to have someone in the workplace.... We want leaders to bust out of the typical paradigm. What we've done is help the church take its rightful and biblical position in the workplace. There's a significant amount of influence in the workplace and the church has been vacant from that. People need to realize that we are all in ministry."

WorkLife Incorporated

This was started out of the vision and calling to provide ALL churches and organizations with the opportunity, ability and tools to equip successfully, resource and commission church members to live out effectively and joyfully their faith at work, no matter where that work is carried out. Today, WorkLife, Inc. serves churches and organizations throughout the United States through a simple yet highly effective system called Maestro, the WorkLife Coaching System which strengthens and gives form to the successful WorkLife models.

This organization was originated by Doug Spada, founder and President of **WorkLife** out of a consistent desire to make a positive contribution. He increasingly found himself involved in sharing the reality of the gospel within the context of daily work and those relationships that come from that environment. Struggling to find the best way to experience personally God's best and deepest calling for his life, Doug looked to his own local church for answers.

Critical Learning

Assuming that joining church staff would be the most significant way to work out his sense of personal calling to serve Christ, Doug set out to do just that. However, this door kept closing and Doug struggled to understand why. This experience contributed to an increasing sense of confusion and frustration concerning Doug's understanding of faith, work and calling. After a challenging period of grappling with this issue, God led Doug to the profound but practical truth that his spiritual gifting had everything to do with his vocational life irrespective of the role or place. Work took on an entirely new perspective as Doug discovered and began to experience the biblical truth that work is a holy calling if done with, for and through a relationship with Jesus Christ. Finally, there was freedom to work as a genuine calling of God.

From Vision to Application

As Doug felt led, he went on a year of prayer focused on seeking how best to assist others like himself, struggling in this area of calling related to faith and work. And what about the local church's role in this? Doug envisioned the tremendous leverage and impact working believers could have on the kingdom of God IF they were equipped and released by their local churches in a sustainable way. Ultimately, it became clear to Doug that God wanted to use him to help local church congregations to both see and actually take up their mandate to help their members practically in this critical area of worklife calling (Eph 4:11-12) - something that had never been done before in a viable way.

As he felt directed, Doug started right where he was, testing in his own local church, Journey Community Church in San Diego CA, he launched the first church-based and congregation-wide WorkLife Coaching System in the United States. In late 2003, **WorkLife** (then known as His Church at Work) began replicating church-based worklife models in other churches. Wooddale Church, a 5,000 member congregation pastored by Dr. Leith Anderson in Eden Prairie, Minnesota was an early example of the success of the WorkLife Impact Methodology. In 2009, the organization name was officially changed from His Church at Work to WorkLife, Inc. Churches of various denominations, size, and age from around the country as well as many companies have been launching the WorkLife Coaching System in partnership with **WorkLife**.

A New Missions Force — Marketplace Missionaries

From the analysis so far, it is true to suggest that one of the challenges before the Church is to equip marketplace missionaries, not just professional missionaries, and that means equipping the whole people of God to reach out to the whole world with the whole gospel of God. Yet, sometimes marketplace Christians are valued by the Church not so much for their marketplace position nor for their calling to serve God in marketplace work, but for the money they can generate to support the professional missionary. These marketplace Christians are encouraged to "partner" with the Church and Missions Agencies who are seeking to reach the lost. Rather than considering this partnership as both parties directly involved in the task, the Church sees the resource potential of Christians in the marketplace as their only contribution. The Church needs to see beyond that to the opportunity for those Christians to be commissioned as marketplace missionaries to reach the nations and teach them through the spheres of commerce, healthcare, education, science, technology, and government. This erstwhile myopic view of failing to recognize the missionary contributions of a huge segment of the body of Christ with tremendous potential to disciple the nations needs to change.

The Full Gospel Businessmen's Fellowship International has a goal of having members in 200 countries. It has been effective in certain parts of Africa since the late 1980s. In Nigeria for example, there are many branches in large cities, especially in the South. Also emerging is the Europartners movement in Europe, and the Christian Business Men's Committee which has members in over 60 countries worldwide. Professional Organizations such as the International Christian Medical and Dental Association and the Nurses Christian Fellowship International are following suit with affiliates in many countries. Christian Enterprise Development Organizations that work with the poor such as the Mennonite Economic Development Associates and Opportunity International are also seeing growth in their membership, especially in developing nations. The foregoing are some Christian organisations whose ministry it is to prepare Christians to work effectively for the Lord in the marketplace. God is on the move in the marketplace and He is calling for Christians to rise up and take their positions as His ambassadors of love to a broken and corrupt world.

Someone recently said that the Martin Luther brought the Word of God back to the people; today, God is taking the work of God back to the people"[20]. Also, as was touched on earlier, it may be relevant to emphasize that to be effective in facilitating marketplace discipleship among Christians, organisations should be interested not only in the spiritual activities of Christians but also in their secular performance in the marketplace. The interest should not polarise to either of the two but should be all embracing as the Lord is interested in the whole man. This means both the secular and the spiritual activities of the individual, the businessman, and the professional.

6

Biblical Examples of Marketplace Servants of the Lord

❧

T hese are some examples of persons in the Bible who were greatly used by the Lord in the various places and circumstances that the Lord placed them.

Paul

The apostle Paul was quite strict in his practice of the Jewish religion when he was originally named Saul. He was very learned, brought up under the teaching of Gamaliel according to the strictness of the Jewish laws (Acts. 22;3), and was extremely eloquent and knowledgeable. He was also a Pharisee and a tentmaker. God personally called Saul and revealed his purpose in life through a divine encounter on his journey to persecute and arrest Christians in Damascus. God struck him blind and he submitted to the Lord as eventually his sight was restored and he was commissioned to the task the Lord had for him. He spent three years in preparation before he met other disciples. Paul's purpose was to bring the gospel to the Gentiles. He was given much divine revelation and God kept him humble to his call. Paul was obedient to his purpose.

It is also relevant to write here that Paul worked for his upkeep. The New Testament records that Paul worked in Galatia, Corinth, Thessalonica, and Ephesus (1 Th. 2:9; 2 Th. 3:7-8; Acts 20:31-35; 1 Cor. 4:12; 9:6). An important text is I Cor. 9 where Paul defends himself against the Judaizers who attacked his apostleship because he worked for a living and did not receive support like the other apostles. Paul first gave the strongest rationale for donor-support in the Scripture and then proceeded to say three times that he made no use of this right and never intended to do so (vv. 12, 15, 18). The Book of First Corinthians was written from Ephesus during Paul's third missionary journey such that the statement covers most of Paul's recorded ministry. In effect, working for a living was Paul's standard operational philosophy. It was also the case that Barnabas also followed this practice even after they split.

Paul made this argument further when he defended his apostleship in the Book of Second Corinthians. He argued that far from undermining his apostleship, his working in order to make the gospel free actually authenticated his apostleship in contrast to the false apostles whose motives were polluted. The cost he paid showed the high value he placed on those he won to Christ. Because he loved them like a father, he wanted to provide for them, rather than they for him (2 Cor. 11:7-11; 12:14-16). In his final comment on this point, Paul stated that he was continuing with this practice (2 Cor. 11: 12). Please note the relevance of this discourse of Paul fending for himself as aptly described in the following statements:

"I have coveted no one's silver, or gold, or apparel. Yes, you yourselves know, that these hands have provided for my necessities, and for those who that were with me" Acts 20:33-34. The relevance is that even in the marketplace, a self-employed professional or entrepreneur who is working, providing professional service or selling some products and earning money for his upkeep, and at the same time working as an evangelist and missionary to spread the gospel is not a novelty. Paul did that many centuries ago.

Abraham

God called Abraham who demonstrated great faith by several acts of obedience to the Lord. He was a rich farmer and shepherd. It is perhaps proper to touch on probably the three strongest demonstrations of his faith in the Lord. The first was when the Lord called him to leave his country, his people, and his family in Ur to Haran, where the Lord promised to bless him and make of him a great nation (Genesis 12: 1- 3). The second was when the Lord promised that he at 99 and Sarah at 90 would have a baby. The Bible records that Abraham believed the Lord and the He counted his faith as righteousness (Genesis 15:6). The third was when he obeyed the Lord's command to go to offer his son, his only son, Isaac (Genesis 22). These three incidents are serious practical issues that a businessman like Abraham handled excellently, passing each test in flying colours. He was a farmer, who was so blessed by the Lord that he became quite wealthy, owning hundreds of sheep and oxen. His history underscores the point that a businessman walking with the Lord, living in obedience to Him, stands to gain and not to lose. The Lord made a covenant with him, promising to bless all the families of the earth through him. This promise has been fulfilled because the Lord Jesus Christ came in flesh, into the world, as a descendant of Abraham.

David

A man after God's own heart, as the Bible describes him (1 Samuel 13:14). He started his life as a shepherd boy who loved the Lord. He also loved his work as a shepherd. Yes, he tried to be an excellent shepherd who was prepared to give his life to protect his sheep as he had to kill a lion and a bear to do so at different times. A God-loving and God-fearing boy under fifteen years of age, showed such courage and dedication in his job that he was inevitably a candidate for higher assignments. "Do you see a man who excels in his work? He will stand before kings. He will not stand before unknown men" Proverbs 22:29. With his performance in his remote background in the fields as a shepherd boy, removed from all human eyes, but not removed from the all-seeing eyes of the Omniscient God, he was a young man to go places. The Lord was convinced that, in David, the same dedication and diligence he showed as a shepherd boy, could be translated as "relevant experience"to the exalted and highly visible position of the king of Israel.

When young David went up against Goliath, he was only a small shepherd boy. King Saul offered David his armour to protect him from the big Philistine, but David knew the weight of the armour would be a hindrance to him. Instead, David used the skills he developed as a shepherd as he was protecting his sheep. A slingshot and stones were his weapons. When the time came for David to exercise his faith in God to slay the giant, he used the skills he had developed. The shepherd fields were David's training grounds. There he learned to fight lions and protect his sheep. Now he would protect God's sheep.

God gives us the same opportunities to develop skills that we shall use to achieve his objectives. However, not all of us will be heroes. Some of us have been called to use our talents to serve others to benefit the kingdom of God. David's faith was the reason God gave him victory. David declared that he came in the name of the living God and that the whole world would know the might of the God of Israel as a result of the defeat of Goliath by a small shepherd boy. This is why God gave him victory over Goliath — so the world may know the living and Omnipotent God.

Yes, he was the king of Israel for many years. He made a number of serious mistakes, but he was God's man; he loved the Lord and knew how to repent and return to the Lord. God saw his heart, his integrity and unparalleled devotion to Him. David could out-dance everyone in his worship of the Lord. A king, yes, and a man attuned to the Lord, he not only danced and wrote psalms but also raised choirs, all for the worship of the Lord. He was not a priest but it is doubtful that there were many priests of his days who outdid him in his worship of the Lord, and in his activities to bring his people to glorify and serve God.

One of the lessons to take away in this section is this: Christian, you do not have to be a priest to praise and worship the Lord. David was not one, but he was so accomplished in praising the Lord that the Bible states that the Lord gave the testimony of him: "I have found David, the son of Jesse, a man after My own heart, who will do all My will" Acts. 13: 22b. Yes, he was a king in the marketplace. Marketplace disciple, this passage in the Bible has been written for our learning and instruction.

Moses

He was born when the Jews in Egypt were being persecuted by a "Pharoh who knew not Joseph". His mother hid him by the river and he was found by Pharoh's daughter and he therefore became an Egyptian prince even though he was a Jew. In the citation made to him in Hebrews 11, the chapter on the "hall of fame" of persons of faith, it is recorded that he preferred to suffer affliction with the people of God to enjoying the pleasures of sin for a season as a prince in Pharoh's palace. He thus exemplifies the personal sacrifice and self-denial that anyone, whether clergy or lay person, has to show in the service of the Lord. Earlier in his life, he made a serious mistake in his zeal by killing an Egyptian who was quarrelling with a Jew, this led to his escape from Egypt into the wilderness where the Lord met and called him.

Timid and fearful when he was called but by the time he completed his assignment of leading his people out of Egypt, he had the courage and bravery which are the makings of only the most successful of army field marshals. Even at the heights of his successes, the Bible records that he was the meekest of men. This contrasts sharply with his brash and overly nationalistic Jewish fervour which was the driving force behind his action that led to his hasty escape from Egypt. Probably another lesson we could learn from this shepherd and leader is that as we work with God to fulfil His purposes through us and with us, He also humbles us to become better persons than we were before our call. That is, inevitably He brings the best out of us.

Joshua

Joshua was chosen by God to bring the people of Israel into the Promised Land after the death of Moses. He is one of our best examples of one who was trained and mentored for a future purpose. He did not know his purpose in the beginning. He was a scout for the Lord's people. For most of his life though he was referred to as the *servant of Moses*. Thus, Joshua modelled servant-hood. Today our society is missing the Joshua's of our day. There are few men and women who are willing to serve others in this way. They often want to be the leader now and fail to learn the important lessons that a mentor can provide. They lack a hunger to learn from older and wiser mentors. This is probably a contributory factor to the multiplicity of churches in the developing world, as each person wants to be a master and leader and not a follower or servant.

Esther

Esther was an orphan and yet a beauty queen. Her uncle Mordecai raised her and she was obedient to him even at the risk of her life in the service of her people as a queen in a foreign land. She was such a beautiful woman that she was chosen to be one of many queens in the king's court. Through circumstances and Godly counsel from her uncle, she discovered that her purpose in life was to save the Jews from extinction. It was a critical moment in history for the young woman who probably struggled with her purpose and identity in life. Her temptation was life-threatening. If she requested audience with the king and he refused, it was a case for being dismissed. Her uncle wisely counselled, "You were made for such a time as this." She stepped through the door of destiny and fulfilled her purpose as she served the Lord even as a beauty queen by stating the Hebrew case against an enemy who sought their extinction.

She was so successful that not only were the Jews saved but also the enemy who sought the extinction of the Jewish people, Haman, was hanged on the gallows that he had made to use against Mordecai

Esther's determination to fast and work for success for the Lord and for her people, the Jews, is eloquently couched in her words: ".....if I perish, I perish" Esther 4:16b. This is an often quoted passage among Christians and we pray that we match our deeds with the determination, to glorify the Lord, that brought forth the words.

Gideon

Gideon was a farmer who was busy doing his work and also trying to avoid persecution from the Midianites. He was threshing wheat when the angel of God came to visit him. He addressed Gideon as a "mighty warrior" which was about as far from the current reality as it could be. Yet, this shows how God views us – He views us in a future tense instead of the current condition. God always sees our potential and sets the course for each of us to fulfil it. Such was the case with Gideon who was called by God to destroy the idols that had been set up in the land. It was a risky business and after the initial dialogue with the Lord, he responded to the call. Gideon, like so many of us, responded to the call just as Moses did and King Saul. "Who am I to do such a thing? I am the least in my family and tribe. I have no skill in this area."

Yet he obeyed the Lord. With his handful of 300 men, he defeated an army of thousands and liberated Israel from the Midianites, Judges: 7.

7

Examples of Modern Marketplace Missionaries and Ministries

ॐ

A few critics of this book have questioned the purpose of this chapter. One has wondered why the author has compiled biographies of individuals. In the introduction of this book, the author wrote that one of the objectives of writing the book is "To present the biographies of modern-day Christians of various professions so that we can learn valuable lessons from their lives". In addition, he explains further:

1. The biographies are for professionals and entrepreneurs who lived for the Lord and were successful in their businesses. Therefore serving and living for the Lord is not a hindrance rather it gets the best out of us including in our professional pursuits.

2. One of the purposes of this book is to show that one can serve the Lord effectively and full-time even in one's accept-

able secular work. Every Christian does not have to become a clergy to serve the Lord full-time. Biographies of Christian professionals who worked full-time for the Lord as they lived doing their secular work should help drive this message home. Reading such biographies provides us with examples of how we could build our lives if in similar or even worse situations. It is a wise person who learns from other people's experience.

3. Two stanzas from A Psalm of Life by Henry Wadsworth Longfellow, 1838, considered relevant are quoted to buttress this point:

"Lives of great men all remind us

We can make our lives sublime,

And, departing, leave behind us

Footprints on the sands of time ;

Footprints, that perhaps another,

Sailing o'er life's solemn main,

A forlorn and shipwrecked brother,

Seeing, shall take heart again".

When we read history and biography, in the author's understanding, one of our reasons is to be challenged by the achievements and experiences of others as long as they are relevant to us in our situations. Such challenges drive us to the point of making breakthroughs in our chosen professions or at the least putting in our best in what we do. With this introduction done, we start with the biography of a great Christian businessman who built a string of retail shops which are now in many big cities of the world. His name was J. C. Penney [22].

J.C. Penney's name was and is still synonymous with "department store." A commentator noted that the life of J. C. Penney "is instructive for business people from all walks of life, particularly Christians". In spite of the "phenomenal success" that he achieved, he never strayed far from his parents' lessons of self-discipline, honour, faith in God, and the Christian ethic of the Golden Rule. He believed in the application of biblical principles not only in his personal life but also in business. The quote on his company's website reads as follows: "Since James Cash Penney opened his first Golden Rule Store in 1902, our goal has been 'to serve the public, as nearly as we can, to its complete satisfaction.' By valuing our customers, associates, communities, investors, products, and services, J C Penney has become one of the most trusted retailers in America" [22]. The store opened in 1902 was his own first Golden Rule Store. Before then, the Golden Rule Store existed as we can see in the following section.

Early Years

James Cash Penney was born on September 16, 1875, on a farm in Caldwell County, near Hamilton, Missouri. He was the seventh of twelve children born to his parents. His father was a poor farmer and a Baptist minister. He spent his childhood doing farm work and attending school. When he was eight, he had to pay for his own clothing as money was scarce and his father wanted him to learn the value of money. He had to raise and sell livestock until neighbours complained of the noise and smell[23].

In 1893, Jim graduated from Hamilton High School and continued to work on the family farm though he really wanted to become a lawyer. Six weeks before he died, Jim's father helped him get a job as a store clerk at a dry goods store in Hamilton. Jim began his training as a salesman on February 4, 1895. The day before he died, his father said prophetically, "Jim will make it. I like the way he has started out." His father's confidence in him was a great source of strength and inspiration throughout his life.

The Golden Rule Stores

J. C. Penney worked hard at the store and the farm. And was often bullied by his colleagues who took customers away from him. He learned that he had to stand up for himself as he gained confidence in himself and developed his skills as a salesman.

He later became ill and was diagnosed as being susceptible to tuberculosis. He had to move to a drier climate. In 1897, he moved to Denver, Colorado, and found work in a dry goods store. Then he bought a butcher shop with all his savings but this first business failed because Penney would not give special favours to a powerful customer.

In 1898, Penney went to work for Thomas Callahan and Guy Johnson, who owned dry goods stores called Golden Rule stores in Colorado and Wyoming. Callahan liked Penney's honesty and strong work ethic. In 1899, he sent Penney to Evanston, Wyoming, to work with Johnson in another Golden Rule store. That same year, Penney married Berta Alva Hess. Then Callahan and Johnson asked Penney to join them in opening a new Golden Rule store. Using money from savings and a loan, Penney joined the partnership and moved with his wife and infant son to Kemmerer, Wyoming, to start his own store.

A Chain of Good Men

The store J. C. Penney opened on April 14, 1902, was a one-room wooden building. He and his family lived in the attic above the store. Penney stocked quality products at fair prices for mining and farm families. He accepted "cash only" for his goods, rather than credit. Penney's store was successful because his customers liked the merchandise and good service.

Within a year, Penney was managing two more stores. Soon, he had a one-third ownership in three stores in Wyoming. By 1907, Callahan and Johnson sold their shares of the chain to Penney who dreamed of starting more Golden Rule stores throughout the West.

The store name represented his religious beliefs and gave him a business motto.

The number of men Penney hired and trained grew larger each year and formed the basis of his company. Penney always called his employees "associates." These men became manager-partners in new stores and also shared in the profits. One of the manager's jobs for each store was to find another honest and hard-working man and train him as manager for another new store. Penney's goal was not to have a chain of stores, but to have a chain of good men. By 1909, Penney established his headquarters office in Salt Lake City.

The J. C. Penney Company

In 1910, tragedy hit. Penney's wife, Berta, died of pneumonia and left him with two sons, Roswell Kemper Penney and James Cash Penney Jr. He was devastated and later wrote that with Berta's death, his "world crashed" around him. Despite his grief, Penney's business continued to prosper. In 1912, there were thirty-four Golden Rule stores with sales surpassing $2 million. The chain name was changed in 1913, becoming the J. C. Penney Company. By 1914, Penney relocated his headquarters to New York City to be closer to the major sources of merchandise.

The J. C. Penney Company flourished under the company motto, "Donor, Confidence, Service, and Cooperation." As new stores appeared across the country, illustrated announcements in newspapers let people know that a J. C. Penney store would soon open in their community. Smart advertising, just treatment of customers, and good products at affordable prices made Penney very wealthy. He opened the first J. C. Penney Store in his home state of Missouri on April 15, 1918, in Moberly.

In 1919, Penney married Mary Kimball. Sadly, she died in 1923, leaving him with another son, Kimball. After Penney's first employer, J. M. Hale, retired in 1924, Penney opened his 500th store in his home-town of Hamilton. Penney bought the same building where he had started his retail career and selected fourteen citizens from Hamilton as his partners in the store. Two years later, Penney married his third wife, Caroline Autenreith. They had two daughters, Mary Frances and Caroline Marie and lived together until his death in 1971.

Good Works and Interests

Throughout his life, Penney reportedly acted in ways that were honest and productive. In the 1920s, the quality of America's dairy and beef cattle was generally poor and he wanted to improve the livestock. He purchased the Emmadine Farm in New York and established a purebred Guernsey herd there. That dairy herd, the Foremost Guernsey Association herd, was given to the University of Missouri in 1952. Penney established a purebred Aberdeen Angus herd. In his father's farm. In addition to establishing farms for cattle, Penney built a residential community for retired clergy. In 1954 he set up the J. C. Penney Foundation. This foundation is said to still support organizations that address important issues such as community renewal, the environment, and world peace.

In his last years, he was a popular speaker and a respected author. He received honorary degrees from a variety of colleges and universities, including the University of Missouri and Stephens College, both in Columbia. James Cash Penney died in New York City on February 12, 1971, at the age of ninety-five.

Ross Bridgend, Making a Difference in Thailand

Ross Bridgend, an Australian, who was attending a business seminar in Thailand when he decided to take a break and walk around the streets, as he did, he had experiences that changed his life[4]. As he walked, he noticed a young boy begging for food and was struck by the fact that he was allowed to be alone on the streets. The little boy took him to his mother, who proudly announced, "My son gets a meal every two days." Later, another woman approached him and offered to sell her two children for the equivalent of 25 dollars. Ross was deeply moved after seeing such desperate poverty. This, combined with a crisis that took place while he was in Thailand in which Ross almost lost his young daughter to an illness, made him rethink his priorities.

On his way back home to Australia, Ross was sitting in the airport when a man came over to introduce himself. Ross shared a little about the plight of the children in Thailand, and the man made a statement that he has never forgotten. "If you have a focus for people less fortunate than yourself, you will never go without a dollar." What made the statement even more profound was because of who it came from — Bill Gates, the founder of Microsoft[24].

When Ross returned home, he could not get the image of the children in Thailand out of his mind. He began to think about ways he could help them. At a seminar, he shared the dilemma of the Thai children with other business leaders and challenged them to consider the purpose for their lives. The attendees gave him $80,000 so he could return to Thailand and begin to change the conditions for these children.

During his second visit, Ross came up with a great idea to fund ongoing aid for orphans and to help people increase their business. Each day he left his hotel, he was approached by one or more tuk-tuk drivers (tuk-tuks are three-wheeled motorcycle taxis). There are about 1,000 tuk-tuks in Chiang Mai, a relatively small city, so competition was fierce. After a few days, he befriended one of the drivers who spoke some English and he learned about his business. Ross asked him if he would like to learn how to increase his revenue by incorporating some simple marketing strategies. The man said yes, so Ross explained that he would help him at no charge if he would be willing to give 10 percent of the increase of his business to help fund the work with the orphans. The man readily agreed. Within a few weeks, his business increased five-fold, and he began contributing to the orphans. That same model has been used to fund the care for over five hundred orphans in Thailand, India and China[4].

Graham Power, a South African Businessman

Graham Power is a successful businessman who became a Christian later in life. God has been using this businessman to bring together men and women from all walks of life in South Africa and other nations inside Africa for a day of prayer. The goal is not just prayer, but transformation of Africa. Stadiums of thousands convene once a year and pray all day.

Charisma magazine featured a story on Graham Power, a successful businessman in Cape Town, South Africa[25]. Graham was awakened one day at 4 am. in July 2000. He said God gave him a vision in three stages. First, he was instructed to rent the 45,000-seat Newlands rugby stadium in Cape Town for a day of repentance and prayer for that city. In the second part of the vision, he saw the prayer movement spreading to the rest of South Africa for a national day of prayer, and in the final part of the vision he saw the effort cover the rest of the continent.

On March 21, 2001, the first step came to pass. A capacity crowd gathered in Newlands stadium for prayer and repentance. Soon after that a notorious gangster in the city was saved.

News of the first gathering spread quickly, and in 2002 eight cities in South Africa hosted the day of prayer. Leading up to the event, young people from all over the country took part in a "Walk of Hope" from Bloemfontein to the eight stadiums where prayer meetings were to be held that year, visiting schools and community centres along the way. The events also were broadcast on television.

Power said he received another vision in February 2002, in which he saw the prayer event in 2003 spreading as far as the widest point in Africa, covering sub-Saharan Africa. The Day of Prayer for Africa in 2003 did exactly that. Not only did 77 cities and towns in South Africa host interdenominational prayer events, but 60 other cities and towns in 27 countries in sub-Saharan Africa also took part.

According to *Charisma*, an estimated 15 million to 30 million Africans from all 53 countries in Africa and five islands gathered for united prayer in hundreds of stadiums throughout the continent" [25]. It all started with the vision of a businessman.

The movement has spread throughout Africa with more countries and stadiums participating in 2003. Graham wants to be a catalyst to bring a positive change to the plight of Africa and especially on the AIDS epidemic. This has grown to a global day of prayer celebrated every year in different cities of the world.

Hotel Owner Transforms His Workplace

Ed Silvoso, author of *Anointed for Business [26]*, tells the story, as contained in this article, of a Philipino business man who owned a hotel chain. God saved this man and began an amazing transformation that led to a major transformation in his large scale hotel. This man owned a 1600 room hotel in three buildings. The hotel had become a haven for prostitution with the rooms being used as many as five times a day. The 2,000 employees had a primary clientèle of prostitutes. There were more than 3,000 prostitutes. One of Silvoso's associates shared with the owner a formula for winning the lost. So, the owner of the hotel went out and hired 40 pastors and told them to follow these instructions:

- Speak peace to the wolves. Bless those who curse you.
- Eat and drink with the sinners. Become their friends.
- Pray for them and their needs.

These were the strict orders. They were not to share the gospel until these three requirements were met for two years. The net result of following these three rules was that all 2,000 employees got saved and the hotel was upgraded to executive level which removed the prostitution because the rates became too high. A prayer chapel was added with 24/7 prayer for anyone by dialling 7 on the telephone. Two years later 10,000 guests had received the Lord on this property. We need to start asking the Lord to help us see how to transform our workplaces today.

Ruth Siemens

This Ruth Siemens' biography has been adapted from an article published by the InterVarsity press [28]. Ruth Siemens, a twentieth century pioneer of tentmaking ministry, who could be described as a marketplace disciple, passed on to glory on December 20, 2005. A month earlier she celebrated her 80th birthday with a gathering of more than 80 family members, friends and former ministry colleagues. Some of these were those she led to the Lord.

While she worked and travelled from country to country, she also went about telling those she met about the Lord. She often invited local residents to after-work gatherings and Bible studies to introduce them to her best friend and Saviour, the Lord Jesus Christ. As she did her secular work, she was also strongly involved in the work of the Lord such that she became a key figure in the growth of the International Fellowship of Evangelical Students (IFES).

She contracted tuberculosis during World War II. As a result, she did not expect to go to the mission field, therefore, she studied Education and English at California State University, Chico, and there she became involved with InterVarsity. It was at the InterVarsity that she learned much about the Lord, including sharing her faith and leading Bible studies. When she became an elementary school teacher after her studies, she continued to share her faith with college students and work with them.

In 1954 she was invited to teach at an international school in Lima, Peru. At this time, Peru was largely unevangelized. But Ruth managed to find a small, evangelical church nearby where she offered to teach a Sunday School class to which she could invite her students. Though she had perfect freedom to preach the gospel in class, she did not do so because it would have violated her educational task. Instead, she freely shared her life in Christ, and invited her students to her Sunday School class. Most of them came and most became believers. In her spare time she conducted classes at the local university to meet students and began a Bible study group for them. After three years, she became an administrator of an elementary school in Brazil and began another student Bible study in her Sao Paulo apartment.

So respected was Ruth in her work, that she revised the curriculum for the whole school during her second year. Ruth also reached out to colleagues through friendship and evangelistic Bible studies such that a number of her colleagues found Christ. Then in her "free" time Ruth went to the university in Lima repeated the same process and started the Peruvian "InterVarsity" movement. Some of the people she led to the Lord have become national and international leaders. Soon the Peruvian movement was going strong and had helped start the Ecuadorian movement and Ruth felt she could move on. So she sent her résumé throughout Spanish-speaking countries in Latin America, but to her surprise, no offer came. So she finally accepted an unsolicited offer from an international school in Brazil to serve as principal. Once again she repeated the same process, winning students, faculty, and staff to Christ and starting the Brazilian "Inter Varsity" movement. In the middle of her work in Brazil, the International Fellowship of Evangelical Students asked Ruth to leave her job, go on support, and give full-time to the student work. So after turning down an offer to double her already good salary, Ruth transitioned from tentmaking to donor-supported ministry. By the time she left Brazil there were student fellowship groups on 30 college campuses. At the invitation of IFES, Ruth then moved to Spain where she pioneered the Spanish and Portuguese university student movements. "Every time I have moved to a different city, God has miraculously provided a place for me to live where students can meet," she wrote in the letter she had prepared for Christmas 2005.

In 1968 IFES asked her to pioneer student work in Spain and Portugal. When she moved to Barcelona, there was no residential housing near the new university campus. She ended up with an apartment one block from the large hospital where she discovered many evangelicals who were training to become doctors and nurses.

Each summer, for six years, she taught evangelism and Bible study at Schloss Mittersill, a 1,000-year old castle in Austria. That led to more training opportunities in France, Switzerland, and then in communist Poland. In 1975 she returned to the U.S. and worked with InterVarsity Missions to promote tentmaking opportunities. In 1976 she began her own organization, "Global Opportunities", to recruit, counsel, train and then provide job referrals for aspiring missionary tentmakers.

In Barcelona she teamed up with Rebecca Manley. Becky was a former InterVarsity staff member, the author of *Out of the Saltshaker*, and now involved in Saltshaker Ministries. Many of the stories shared in *Out of the Saltshaker* occurred in Ruth's Barcelona apartment. Later they wrote the book on "Evangelism – A way of life" together.

Becky wrote a letter to Ruth for her 80th birthday that included these words:

"I came to Spain as a college student and a young convert to Christ. ... You detected that I'd never led a person to Christ before and told me how. But it was far more than skills that I gained. In observing you I saw what a walk of faith looked like up-close. Everything you thought, felt, delighted in, or regretted was viewed in relationship to the Living God. Your relationship to Christ was one of such delight and awe that it was impossible to understand you unless one knew the God that you worshipped. And that, I believe, is your ultimate epitaph. Your life has been a clarion call to everybody you ever encountered that we must give our lives unreservedly to Christ – for it is only in radical surrender to Him that we find our true joy and freedom".

Martin Butterworth

BMS engineer **Martin Butterworth was** honoured by his Nepali colleagues at Nepal Hydro and Electric (NHE) on January 29th 2004 as he stepped down after seven years engineering work at the power company[29]. Colleagues and friends at NHE presented Martin with a plaque commending him for his contribution over the last seven years in Nepal. After much prayer and consideration, Martin stood down from his position as quality manager, but importantly, he had trained a Nepali colleague to take on his responsibilities.

In recent years, NHE has expanded significantly in terms of its volume of manufactured work and the breadth of its services and skills. NHE makes electrical and mechanical equipment for the hydropower industry and employs around 140 people, one-third of whom are skilled tradesmen, with about 50 apprentices from the Butwal Technical Institute (BTI) who work in the factory for practical training and expertise.

Martin played a key role in the development of the Quality Management System at NHE, which has helped it grow to be one of the leading engineering companies in Nepal. Liz Russell, BMS regional secretary for Asia, said, "Over the past seven years at NHE, Martin has done an excellent job in an extremely challenging working environment. He has demonstrated the value of witness by Christian professionals in a secular or other-faith environment."

Martin, along with his wife Katrina, a medical doctor, and their two young daughters Ruth and Esther, have their home church in Shipley Baptist Church, West Yorkshire, England. The Butterworths live in Kathmandu, Nepal, where Katrina is a medical co-ordinator for the BMS partner United Mission to Nepal and works at Patan Hospital.

The Marketplace Ministries Movement

Most of the organisations touched on in this section and even in the next chapter are overseas-based, indeed, mainly US based. One of the reasons for doing this is to present to Christians in developing countries some of the organisations which they could emulate by starting similar ministries in their nations. It is useful that we could learn from the experience of others who are ahead of us as we seek to serve the Lord in the marketplace.

Some of the large ministries are the Christian Business Men's Committee, the International Christian Chamber of Commerce, Fellowship of Companies for Christ International, the C12 Group, and the Christian Management Association (CMA). Growth in CMA exemplifies the experience of many of these ministries, accelerating from a handful of members in 1976 to over 3,500 chief executive officers, business owners, middle managers, pastors, and church administrators representing more than 1,500 organizations. Whereas these larger ministries seek to provide a full-service training and fellowship experience to members, many other faith-at-work ministries are primarily event-driven, usually offering prayer breakfasts or a speaker series. An example of the smaller ministries is that of Bill Leonard, a real estate executive in Atlanta, who decided to reach out to the hi-tech community by sponsoring a once-a-year "High Tech Prayer Breakfast" in Atlanta. Every October, leaders in the high-tech community come to hear an inspirational talk that usually has a salvation message in it. Table sponsors bring business associates as a means of introducing seekers to Christ. More than 1,500 were in attendance in one of the past years. This has led to other such events in the real estate and financial services industries.

8

Some Frequently Asked Questions and Suggested Answers on Marketplace Discipleship, and Some Examples of Marketplace Evangelism.

ॐ

Q: How would you define workplace ministry?

A: According to Os Hillman[30], Workplace ministry is an intentional focus of equipping men and women in all spheres of work and society to understand and experience their work and life as a holy calling from God.

Q: Doesn't a job leave too little time and energy for spiritual ministry?

A: The question assumes you serve God only in free time. But Christians are to *integrate* work and witness. Their ministry is *full-time*. Every day they *live out* the Gospel and share it at every chance they get. Their work provides the platform for natural contacts. Their integrity, quality work, caring relationships and well chosen comments about God cause seekers to ask questions without arousing hostility in others.

Q: Is it fair to employers to evangelize at work?

A: Employers *benefit* from faithful Christians. The Christians' first concern is personal integrity, quality work and caring relationships. Paul taught converts that we are to serve our employer as the Lord Himself (Eph. 6:5-8, Col. 3:23-25). What pleases God usually pleases the boss. A contract with him is a contract with God. To spend daily time with non-believers implies spiritual responsibility. Silence is never an option. Our secular work itself glorifies God, but it is no substitute for sharing the Good News. To avoid witness at work (to minimize risk), in order to evangelize elsewhere, will backfire. Lifestyle evangelism cannot be switched on and off. However, we need to ensure that we do not shelve our assignments and start talking to our colleagues about the Gospel. We should ensure that we carry our secular assignments conscientiously, as unto the Lord. That is also a part of our witness.

Living Out at Faith in the Marketplace[31]

66 "Y ou are our letter, written in our hearts, known and read by all men" II Cor. 3:2. This write-up is taken from the article by Dennis Peacocke as given in the Reference.

He suggests that the best way to evangelize anyone anywhere is simply to live out our faith. He continues: "Our most effective witness as individuals, a church, or a company is to embody evangelism as a lifestyle rather than a contrived program. People sense the difference between the authenticity of our love for them in Christ and our targeting them as part of our "soul-winning" endeavours. As in all things, only the real deal works."

He points out the following four major issues surrounding effectively sharing our faith at work:

1. Our faith and worship must be demonstrated through our work.
2. More than words, our lives witness to our faith.
3. Loving people necessitates bringing God into our conversation with them.
4. All of us must be trained and constantly growing in our skills of "fishing" for men and women.

Let us now examine each of these critical issues in order.

Our Faith and Worship Must Be Demonstrated through Our Work

Dennis suggests that most Christians believe that the word "worship" describes something we do at church services when we join the congregation in singing, but "worship" means much more than that. He submits that: "To worship God means to reverence

Him, honour Him, and submit our lives to Him". In other words, "to worship God is to posture ourselves in reverence before Him in the totality of all we do in life. Worship is then a lifestyle, in the Christian reality, and true worship draws the Holy Spirit into any activity or environment".

He continues: "As I point out in my book, *Doing Business God's Way*, work is a holy, eternal calling. Therefore, our work should be an act of worship before our Master who ordained it to be so. To "evangelize" is to invoke the presence of God into the interaction of human beings, especially among the yet unsaved". If then, my work is done self-consciously as an act of faith and worship, I can expect God's presence in it. "Our first form of evangelism in the workplace, or anywhere else, is the incarnating of God's pleasure in our obedient, excellent work as a demonstration to all men of the manifest reality of His presence in our life".

More Than Our Words, Our Lives Witness to Our Faith

"Since most adults spend more time at work than anywhere else, it is my conviction that the workplace ought to be the most opportune setting for believers to draw others into their eternal destiny in God. It is the "evangelistic" context with the greatest potential. It is precisely for this reason that our spiritual enemy has made the workplace "off limits" to the church in terms of adequately training people how to successfully display Christ there" Dennis says.

He focuses on the problem of Christians being inadequately trained by the church such that we fail to be effective as witnesses for the Lord because it is at work where we spend most of our time that people can see through and know us as we really are. His words: "At work, people see the real us; they read our faces more than our tracts and listen to our soulish nonsense more than our "religious conviction." If we're not "living our faith at work," no other "witness" sufficiently counteracts the real us we have put on display. It is for this reason I am so excited about the Holy Spirit's growing focus on Christ in the marketplace. It is going to force millions of believers to put up or shut up or at least shut up until they grow up".

Loving People Necessitates Bringing God into Our Conversations with Them

He suggests that "Real love, rather than duty-driven "religious love," mandates that believers live their faith enough to legitimize their verbal sharing of it. If you love me, show me; then tell me. Our grand problem as believers is that we simply love ourselves more than our neighbour or, in this case, our co-workers".

He says that "Christian business" does not just mean that one is "basically honest, pays one's taxes, has some Bible verses on the wall, and no Playboy magazines in the men's room, no cigar", etc. He suggests that "Christian business" should mean more; it should mean showing the love of Christ and the living out of His law-word principles as it is made to permeate the business from top to bottom.

It should mean the law of love in the heart of believers which covers people in prayer and seeks non-plastic ways to share God's love, life, and gospel with them. He suggests that "we should be praying and seeking ways to find genuine opportunities to demonstrate and speak the truths of the gospel with those in the workplace – ways they can see and with words that don't reek of religious platitudes or preachy superiority".

All of Us Must Be Trained and Constantly Growing in Our Skills of "Fishing" for Men and Women

He reminds us that "Jesus told Peter in Matthew 4:4, and by implication to all believers, that He would make Peter a "fisher of men." Fishing requires skill and a great deal of focused attention if one wants to be truly successful. As a general rule, Christians tend to be lousy fishermen".

He drives home his point as he uses contrasts to show the difficulty believers face in successfully getting into public conversation. This author has listed out the contrasts that Dennis gives in his writing. They are as follows:

1. The world is having a conversation, and we aren't in it because unbelievers are not focusing on what we believers want them to be discussing.
2. The world is talking about economic security and prosperity; we want them to be talking about their after-lives.

3. They are talking about taxes and education; we want them to be talking about the scriptures.

4. They are talking about job security, crime, and education; we want them to be talking about Jesus, heaven, and the anti-Christ!

He concludes by suggesting the way forward that should enable us as Christians to be more effective. He says:

1. "Let's deal with it, Christians, you catch fish using their food (bait), not the food we want them to be feeding on! In order to fish with bait the world's fish are biting on, it will require believers to do a glorious thing.

2. We must study what the scriptures say about crime, education, taxation, national defence, building successful relationships, and economic prosperity deeply enough to intelligently get into their conversation and evangelize like Jesus did.

3. We must practice spiritual jujitsu (Japanese unarmed combat) and use what people give us of themselves and their real concerns and then gently lead them in the direction of Christ using those concerns.

4. This kind of biblical evangelism in the marketplace will not only "catch" the attention of the unbelievers, it will impact and transform believers in remarkable ways. We will actually learn the scriptures as they relate to here-and-now-reality and how God wants to release His Kingdom and will on earth as it is in heaven, prior to Christ's return".

In conclusion, he suggests:

1. "The Spirit of God is pressing the issue of understanding biblical, economic realities and the ministry of believers in the workplace with a powerful and growing insistence. This necessitates a much deeper knowledge of the scriptures, a fundamental change in the way local churches equip their people for broad-based ministries, and a much more elective level of general evangelism".

2. He concludes: "Martin Luther ushered in the revelation of the *priesthood* of all believers, and now the Holy Spirit, using the marketplace, is ushering in the *ministry* of all believers! Go, God!"

9

Transforming a City for Christ through the Marketplace

༄

C an a city be transformed for Jesus Christ? This sounds like such a lofty goal that few will ever seek to attain it. In his article, Os Hillman writes that today we are finding no less than 200 cities across the world that are in some form of transformation in the world, according to Alistair Petrie, author of *Transformed![32]* Petrie spoke at the 2004 ICWM Workplace Transformation Summit in Minnesota October 26, 2004. He cited these cities as having a level of transformation in every aspect of its public and governmental and business life. This is what it means to transform. It could be defined as: "change the form of; to change in structure or composition; to change in nature, disposition, heart, or the like; convert. It means a thorough or radical change, whether in appearance or nature." However, transformation does not mean perfection for either an individual or city. We shall discuss some Christian professionals that the Lord has used in city transformation. We, Christians in developing countries, need to study the activities of these Christians even as we pray to the Lord to heal our nations. In the twenty first century, if ever there are nations that need transforming, ours in the developing world should come to the fore. This is not saying that nations in developed world are perfect and acceptable to the Lord, they are not and indeed, no country has all its people living morally acceptable lives before the Lord.

However, it is not only that we in the developing world are not living right, it is also that we are guilty of corruption and mismanagement of resources to such an extent that many of our people live in poverty and squalor in spite of the natural resources with which God has blessed us. Our poverty is so bad that we are a problem to the developed world. We are focus of their concern and object of their pity such that the United Nations instituted the Millennium Development Goals, being initiatives aimed at helping countries in developing countries. International donor agencies invest fund and aid continually on developing countries. We need the salvation of the Lord to rescue us from spiritual, moral and physical poverty. Therefore, national transformation should be one of the goals worth pursuing by marketplace disciples from developing countries as we pray that the Lord will heal our nations.

Dawie Spangenberg, Director of Transformation Africa exhorts business leaders in a city to take seriously their commitment to their city. He said in a talk to marketplace leaders, "If you are a businessman or woman in your city and you are not actively involved in using your talent and resources to transform your city then you are raping your city"[33]. This statement contains a strong language but there is truth to it. Our businesses were not made simply to provide employment and a good living for all those involved in that business. There is a higher purpose that God has for any business. We must be good stewards of that calling upon our work lives. We now take a look at the story of Jeremiah Lanphier, a man the Lord used in New York.

Jeremiah Lanphier: One man's obedience to prayer... began a revival...that transformed a nation[34].

*Jeremiah Lanphier was a busita*nessman in New York City who asked God to do something significant in his life. He was a man approaching mid life without a wife or family, but he had financial means.

Following his heart desire to reach the neediest around him, he put aside his regular business and began to work with the North Dutch Church in Manhattan as a lay missionary. At that time, there were 30,000 men idle on the streets of New York. Drunkenness was rampant, and the nation was divided by slavery. Ministering in the dark slums, Lanphier poured himself into the lives of people who were homeless, helpless and hopeless. Month after month he went door to door sharing the Good News, distributing tracts, and holding Bible studies with whomever would listen.

In a small darkened room, in the back of one of New York City's lesser churches, he prayed alone. His request of God was simple, but earth-shattering: "Lord, what wilt Thou have me to do?" He made a decision to reject the "success syndrome" that drove the city's businessmen and bankers. God used this businessman to turn New York City's commercial empire on its head.

Lanphier would begin each day going from office to office, house to house, and shop to shop; but by midday he was physically, emotionally and spiritually worn out. He discovered that, even as the body needs food, the soul and spirit need prayer. Lanphier realized his need and regularly returned to a room in the church Consistory building to cry out to God for spiritual strength. This fresh, personal experience of the power of prayer suggested to Lanphier that there might be others, especially those engaged in business, who might profit from time in prayer. He handed out some 20,000 flyers advertising the first noonday prayer meeting on September 23, 1857. He was equipped by the church in Foulton Street to begin a businessmen's prayer meeting on that day.

For the first thirty minutes he sat alone praying. Eventually, steps were heard coming up the staircase and another joined. Then another and another until Lanphier was joined by five men. The next Wednesday the six increased to twenty. The following week there were 40. Lanphier and the others then decided to meet daily, and within weeks thousands of business leaders were meeting for prayer each day. Before long over 100 churches and public meeting halls were filled with noonday prayer meetings. God moved so powerfully that similar prayer meetings sprang up around the nation. For a season there were 10,000 conversions to Christ each week in New York City, and it is estimated that nearly one million people across the U.S. were transformed during this incredible move of God. *The New York Tribune* and the *New York Herald* issued articles of revival. It had become the city's biggest news. Now a full-fledged revival, it moved outside New York. By spring of 1858, 2,000 met daily in Chicago's Metropolitan Theatre, and in Philadelphia, the meetings mushroomed into a four-month long tent meeting. Meetings were held in Baltimore, Washington, Cincinnati, Chicago, New Orleans, and Mobile. Thousands met to pray because one man stepped out. Annus Mirabilis, the year of national revival, had begun. This was an extraordinary move of God through one man. It was unique because the movement was led by businessmen, a group long considered the least prone to any form of evangelical fervour, and it had started on Wall Street, the most unlikely of all places to begin. The result was more than 1 million people coming to Christ. .

Other laypersons that the Lord used, not in the same scale as Lanphier, are discussed in the following paragraphs. They include Nan Jarvis, and Dennis and Megan Doyle. The Doyles were really involved in supporting Christian organisations.

Nan Jarvis

Nan was born into a family of nine children, and her father committed suicide when she and her twin sister were just three and a half in South Africa[35]. She was reportedly sexually abused by her uncles, raped and physically abused even by her own husband. She came to know the Lord Jesus Christ personally during this time. After three years of marriage and then divorce, she and her son, Richard, moved to Swaziland. Instead of wallowing in self pity and becoming a victim of her circumstances, Nan trusted the Lord.

Swaziland is a nation of one million people that leads the world in the number of HIV/AIDS cases, with more than 50 percent of the population infected. God used Nan as a catalyst for transformation in this small nation. The country is a monarchy heavily steeped in tribal ways. Nan owned a flower shop and decided to deliver flowers to the king's five queens' households as they were then. As she was preparing the first flower arrangements, she felt that the Holy Spirit directed her to make the deliveries herself which she did.

This opened doors for her to get into people's homes, hospitals, clinics, schools, government offices, parliamentary houses and even into the king's palaces, where she has had many opportunities to be a witness, share the gospel, pray for people and see the hand of God touch and heal many lives. Swaziland is a nation with deeply held tribal traditions, such as polygamy and sexual immorality, and erroneous foundations laid by their forefathers, such as ancestral worship and witchcraft. However, with time, Nan developed a relationship with many of the king's wives. One of these wives in particular eventually gave her life to the Lord and was filled with the Holy Spirit. This queen's life radically changed over the years such that she has implemented many things within her sphere of influence that have expressed her new-found faith. For example, she is promoting gospel music in the nation and has her own choir called "Redemption." The king, queen mother and many of the other queens and leaders of the nation are professing Jesus Christ as Lord. On a personal note, the queen earned a law degree and has been admitted into the law court of the nation. Nan remains in a close relationship with the royal family, interceding on their behalf as they bring about positive change to the nation. They are a nation undergoing a tremendous warfare for survival spiritually, socially and economically. The minister of Health and Social Welfare called for national prayer and repentance for the AIDS pandemic. Nan's personal life and the struggles which she has overcome greatly prepared her for the "Joseph" role she is playing in this country. She has become a spiritual and physical provider to this nation. She has become a catalyst to bring agricultural programs into the nation through the ICCC and other groups. She has prayed and seen God send the rain that allowed people to eat once again. She believes that the Lord has told her that Swaziland will become a "bread basket nation" and that it will feed itself and other nations. Nan is now in the medical profession, and sees God doing many mighty miracles in her daily marketplace. She is a practical example of how God can heal a broken heart and use it tin the transformation of a nation.

Dennis and Megan Doyle are committed believers who own one of the largest commercial real estate companies in Minnesota[36].

In 1995, the Doyle's established a private foundation in order to support a wide range of non-profit charities more effectively. The ministry is Hope for the City, which they started in 2000. It gathers corporate surpluses and distributes them to approximately eighty-five qualified non-profit organizations, primarily in the Twin Cities area. These organizations then distribute the surpluses to the poor. When The Kingdom Oil Christian Foundation (KOCF) started in Minneapolis in 2003, as an affiliate of The National Christian Foundation (NCF), the Doyles closed their private foundation and transferred the assets to a KOCF Giving Fund. As a result, over the next several years the Doyles gained numerous major advantages which included the following:

- They saved hundreds of thousands of dollars in income taxes, because they could receive tax deductions for up to 50 percent of their adjusted gross income on contributions they made to their Giving Fund, compared to only 30 percent with their private foundation.

- They saved tens of thousands of dollars because their Giving Fund is exempt from excise taxes, while private foundations must pay excise taxes of 2 percent of net investment income earned.

- They shed themselves of many of the burdens of operating a private foundation and turned over virtually all administrative responsibilities to KOCF. For example, the Doyles saved time and effort, as well as considerable accounting and legal fees, because they no longer had to file the annual tax returns required for private foundations.

- They gained the ability to give anonymously because their Giving Fund information is kept private, whereas private foundations' IRS 990 forms are subject to public record searches.

"I couldn't believe the excellent support we received from Kingdom Oil," recalls Dennis. "I had a particularly complex situation, because I owned a large amount of real estate investment trust (REIT) stock that I had acquired through a tax deferred exchange. Restrictions prevented me from liquidating it for approximately three years. So I contributed the REIT stock to my Giving Fund and received a fully substantiated fair market value tax deduction."

It was mutually beneficial to both parties, a win-win situation. The Giving Fund received money that it could give away to charities while the Doyles saved several hundred thousand dollars in income taxes in the year of the donation.

As a result, far more than the Doyle's original contribution became available for the Lord's work. While the REIT stock resided in the Giving Fund awaiting the lapse of the restrictions, it appreciated 45 percent and paid out numerous dividends. The Doyles paid no capital gains tax on the stock appreciation and no income tax on the dividend income allocated to their Giving Fund.

Dennis and Megan have continued to donate to their Giving Fund on a regular basis, including additional REIT stock contributions five times greater than their original contribution in 2003. "I'm a great believer in contributing appreciated stock rather than cash," says Dennis. "We get an income tax deduction for the full appreciated value in the year of our donation, and we incur no capital gains tax liability on the amount of the appreciation. Once the money is in the Fund, we can take time to carefully choose the ministries we want to support as the assets in our Giving Fund appreciate tax-free."

10

Failures of Christians as
Marketplace Disciples

ૐ

A mong some Christians, particularly in developing countries, there is the notion that it takes one working as a cleric to be fully involved in the Lord's work. The statement that one is in "full-time ministry in the Church" is often interpreted as meaning that one is in the clergy. Moreover, the multiplicity of churches in developing countries appears to lend credence to the thinking that it is only when we are pastors and ministers of religion that we are in full-time ministry. In other words, if we are not in the clergy, we are not in the Lord's full-time service.

Another failing that apparently stems from a wrong conception of the sacred-secular dichotomy is in the form of different behaviours at different places by the same individual Christian. For example, some Christians behave differently when at church and at the marketplace. At church, they put on their best of behaviours but at work or in business, they behave like any other person.

This explains why in some developing countries, or states in developing countries where most of the population are Christians, on Sunday mornings, most homes in cities are deserted because almost everyone is at church. In those areas, one may find no shops open. Such is the zeal to go to church that close to ninety percent of the population are busy, singing, dancing, or praying at church. In spite of this, some of the countries are the most corrupt in the world. This observation begs the question: what is the impact of the Christian message and Gospel on us since the behaviours of most church-goers and non-church-goers are the same? It is true to say that if it is only the non-church-goers that are guilty of crimes and corruption, these countries will not be as bad as they are.

Example of Marketplace Failures

Researchers conducted a survey among various workers and employees in some cities. They measured a wide range of moral and ethical behaviours which included some of the following:

- Calling in sick when not sick,
- Cheating on income tax,
- Pilfering company supplies for personal use, etc.
- Doing personal work during office hours,
- Reading the Bible and doing personal Bible studies during office hours,

- Using company property and /or time to prepare religious or town's meetings assignments such as reports, accounts, minutes of meetings, invitations, etc.
- Absence from work or skiving during office hours with false excuses,
- Misusing company time and property by doing personal studies not relevant to company tasks during office hours,
- Applying for other jobs using company time and property, etc.

The results of the survey were disappointing. What the researchers found most startling was that there was no significant difference between the churched and the unchurched in their ethics and values on the job. In other words, despite the fact that more and more people attend churches, churches seem to be having less impact on the behaviour of their people, at least in the workplace. To quote the researchers:

"These findings...will come as a shock to the religious leaders and underscore the need for religious leaders to channel the new religious interest in America not simply into religious involvement but in deep spiritual commitment."

The original survey was conducted in the United States. It is also necessary to explain that the list above is not original. It has been modified and increased with conducts and failings observed in workers in developing countries. While it is correct to state that this survey has not been conducted in any city in a developing country, it should be realistic to suggest that if it is carried out, worse results will be recorded. This is because such a survey should serve as a "barometer" to measure our behaviours based on the listed parameters. We already know that our behaviours are full of failings and short comings of which we need to repent as will be shown in the later paragraphs of this chapter. This is why far worse results will be recorded of our ethical behaviours.

Norman Tebbit's Cricket Loyalty Test, Soccer Test, Mammon Test

"For where your treasure is, there will your heart be also", Mathew 6:21.

This passage in Matthew is used by the Lord to show where the loyalty of a person lies. This could be similar to the Norman Tebbit's "Cricket Loyalty Test". He suggested in April 1990 that immigrants and their children could not show loyalty to Britain until they supported the England team at cricket. "A large proportion of Britain's Asian population fail to pass the cricket test. Which side do they cheer for? It's an interesting test. Are you still harking back to where you came from or where you are" he said in an interview with the los Angeles Times. [John Carvel, The Guardian, Thursday 8 January 2004]

In the same way, one could ask a UK citizen from Nigeria whether he would support UK or Nigeria if the two countries were playing a football or soccer match?

Perhaps a more relevant test that we should pose to ourselves as individual Christians in developing countries is the Mammon Test. Some of the relevant scenarios could be as follows:

1. As a businessman, will he be prepared to close his eyes or get involved in cutting corners in order to win a lucrative contract?

2. As a trader, will he sell questionable goods or short-change his customers? (There was a time that this writer bought items from a trader in a developing country. As he was leaving the trader's stall, he was recalled by the trader to collect his change which he had forgotten. The trader showed honesty.)

3. As a church member, will the Christian obtain money incorrectly from any source, pocket or use some, and give some to the church?

4. As a contractor, will he receive money from a customer for a project and use it judiciously as agreed with him?

These questions are not theoretical but based on experiences of Christians in some developing countries. The experiences include the following:

1. A senior church member, well known as a Christian, refused to pay overdue house rents as a tenant in a house owned by a younger Christian. He was reluctant to pay even after being

reported to a more senior Christian. The tenant claimed that his landlord was very well employed and earning good salary. Besides, he was in a position to help him obtain a contract with his multinational employer but had not given him any. How did he expect him to pay the rent when he had not helped him find projects and contracts?

2. There are many stories and allegations of Christian contractors and businessmen accepting money from fellow Christians on building projects. After some months, the contractors come up with stories that the money, the two parties agreed to initially, is no longer adequate to complete the project. Sometimes, the contractors may not even offer any explanations but just abandon the projects. The owner of the project may start pleading with other Christians to intervene to get the contractor give an account or restart the project. This allegation takes many forms. Sometimes, it is claimed that the contractor may take a photograph of another completed house and send to the owner if he is overseas. It is only when he returns to the country that he finds out that the photographed house is not his own but another person's.

3. It is sad that some Christian businessmen readily and happily accept jobs and payments from other Christians only to fail to deliver. Some of these businessmen owe their Christian customers for years without making efforts to repay. Sometimes, the Christian customers are compelled to write off the debts as bad debts when it becomes obvious that the businessmen are not

bothered to repay the debts. What should not be lost to Christian contractor, businessman, and customer is that each person is accountable to the Lord. Being faithful to each other is actually being faithful to the Lord. For, whatever we do as Christians, we should do to the glory of the Lord.

Another point, which is more worrying, could be couched as a question. It is this: if the Christian businessman and contractor can afford to fail their Christian brethren who are their customers, how do they behave to non Christians? Is it likely that they behave differently to the unbeliever than they behave to their Christian brethren? Not quite, they do not behave any differently because their behaviour of failing to keep to agreement is what the unbeliever practises normally. What therefore the Christian contractor or businessman is doing is to carry over the failings in the marketplace to the church. This is why the Mammon Test is necessary. Each Christian, businessman, contractor, employee, employer, etc., should ask themselves whether they are being faithful to the Lord or bowing to Mammon because of the attraction and love of money. How can we be used as disciples in the marketplace if and when we are guilty of dishonesty in business? Where is our testimony? If we shall be the disciples that we should be, we need to repent and try to meet our obligations to our customers whether they are Christians or not. This should help us walk with the Lord effectively.

It may be relevant to call up a present day example. An example of a family business whose founder saw both times of prosperity, and later adversity, and even bankruptcy as a result of refusal to compromise on biblical principles. In the short term, they suffered in their determination to honour the Lord by refusing to give bribe as commanded in the word of God. In the long run, it is now one of the most successful businesses of its type in the world. Its current description is that: "it has grown into one of the largest and most profitable ski and wakeboard boat manufacturers in the world, winning six consecutive J.D. Power Associates Awards and three consecutive NMMA Customer Satisfaction Index awards". It is the Correct Craft Company founded by Walter C. Meloon.

Walter C. Meloon and Sons, and Correct Craft

Walter C. Meloon was born in 1893 and brought his family to central Florida in 1925. That year he founded the Florida Variety Boat Company which in 1936 became Correct Craft. Correct Craft boats were featured in the first water-ski show and tournament. During World War II Correct Craft produced 400 boats for the Army, all ahead of schedule. For this, the company was awarded the Army and Navy "E" award in 1945. The company introduced Ski Nautique in 1951, revolutionizing the industry. In April 2000, Correct Craft celebrated its 75th anniversary, making it the oldest family-owned and operated boat manufacturer in the world. Walter C. Meloon died in

1974. His Great Floridian plaque is located at Correct Craft, Inc., 5717 South Orange Avenue, Orlando [37].

Perfecting the Craft

The Meloon family built up a family business that has stood for Christian ethics in belief and action through both times of prosperity and adversity. In each of these experiences, they remained faithful to God and have inevitably left a legacy of inspiration and hope for Christian businesspeople everywhere who are facing the possibility of business failure or tough decisions.

Correct Craft

Correct Craft, their boat manufacturing business, was started in two garages as a hobby and vision in 1926 by W.C. Meloon. Sadly those two garages burned in separate fires within the period of one year. Walter, a faithful Baptist believer, was influenced in his business principles by his reading of New England Puritans, so he worked for five years to repay his suppliers, bank, and customers. Through his dedication, he passed on those biblical principles he had learned from the Puritans to the next generation, who later ran the business and faced many more difficulties.

No Work on Sunday

One of the best examples of Meloon's biblical approach to business was his refusal to work on Sundays. During World War II,

General Eisenhower needed boats to be built in two weeks so that the Allied Forces could cross the Rhine River. Some sources put the number at 700 boats in two weeks[38]. Another source has it that on February 9, 1945, General Eisenhower needed 1,200 boats to be ready for the attack to be launched on March 10[th][39].

The normal work schedule of Meloon and his company was building 48 boats per month. However, he said that they would build 300 boats for the military in two weeks. Other boat companies would provide the remaining necessary boats. The difference between Correct Craft and the other companies was that Correct Craft refused to work on Sundays to meet the deadline, while others did. It was reported that the U.S. Army tried to force Correct Craft to keep building through the Lord's Day but Meloon simple said "no" because he intended to do the job to glorify God, and the Bible commands that we remember the Sabbath. He told the Army colonel in charge of negotiations that they would turn down the contract if they were required to work on Sundays, and finally the colonel agreed to the exception.

So Meloon kept to his word to provide the boats in only six production days per week. At the deadline, the other boats contractors fell short of their quota and, in addition, their boats did not meet the specifications that the military had provided, so those vessels could not be used. Correct Craft, on the other hand, had met the deadline early and their boats were the only ones built according to specs. The government was so pleased that they asked Correct Craft to build another boat before the deadline was up, and so they did. Later the government called it a miracle and honoured them with the Army and Navy "E" award, and it reportedly went into the records as "the miracle production."

Refusal to Give Bribe

Later, when his sons took over the company and continued to apply God's Word to their business, they ran into some problems in spite of their faithfulness to the Lord. As they were working on another government project, the Meloons refused to dishonour God by paying solicited bribes to government officials. In retaliation, the officials rejected several boats built by Correct Craft even though their specifications were correct. Their refusal to give in to the easy decision to bribe the officials led to the rejection of 600 boats. As a result, Correct Craft went into bankruptcy. In spite of that, they paid off their creditors notwithstanding their legal absolution, and worked relentlessly for 19 years until every creditor was paid in full. This experience is discussed again later in the last paragraph.

Christian Principles

Today, Correct Craft continues to run on Christian values and is one of the leading boat manufacturing companies in the country with their well-known "Nautique" line of sport boats. His oldest son, Walter O. Meloon, (W.O., hereafter) upheld the tradition established by his father of "building boats to the glory of God," . He always dreamed of great things and was instrumental in the company becoming part of organized water-skiing. As Correct Craft, Inc., the company is an innovative leader in the ski and wakeboard boat manufacturing industry.

He was a man of vision with a love for sales and design. He started as a young boy from school and worked his way up the ladder holding such lofty positions as Vice President and President for Correct Craft. His vision and initiative to keep Correct Craft afloat during turbulent financial times resulted in the creation of Midwest Correct Craft, New England Correct Craft, and Mid-Atlantic Correct Craft. He was the first person in the boat industry to organize dealer meetings. These types of meetings were common in the automobile industry but not in the boat industry.

He started the expansion of their manufacturing facility to Plant 1 and later to another site known as Plant 2 under the leadership of his brother. He also brought in a full time chaplain and held regular devotional services for Correct Craft employees. These are just a few of the achievements W.O. accomplished to help the company and keep his father's dream alive. On Monday March 21st 2005, at the age of 89, W.O. Passed away[40].

Current Status

Over time, it has grown into one of the largest and most profitable ski and wakeboard boat manufacturers in the world, winning six consecutive J.D. Power Associates Awards and three consecutive NMMA Customer Satisfaction Index awards.

From inception, Correct Craft operated under simple yet profound philosophies: integrity, ingenuity and servitude – a mission that still stands true today. Now situated in its new 217,000-square-foot corporate headquarters on 138 acres of land in east Orlando, Correct Craft could play off its well-known "Nautique" brand name and operational methods that have worked well enough in the past to make it a multimillion-dollar company with $117 million in annual sales and 450 employees.

In 1959, the company filed for Chapter11 after a government contract for 3,000 boats was pulled. According to the family, a government inspector began rejecting large numbers of boats after Correct Craft refused to carry his expense account even though he was already being compensated by the government – what one might call "double-dipping." With the contract cancelled and $1 million in debt, Correct Craft reduced its workforce from 500 to 25, filed Chapter 11 and began recovery efforts. Six years of bankruptcy negotiations resulted in creditors agreeing to 10 percent owed to them in addition to the 10 percent Correct Craft had already paid to them. In turn, Correct Craft could remain operational. While this story may sound all too familiar, the ending to this tale is far from typical. Steadfast in honour and Biblical principles, the Meloon family committed to paying back the entire 100 percent principle on their debt. Every few extra dollars each week went to creditors, and after years past by, they began paying off widows of creditors who had died. In 1984, the Meloons had finally reached their goal and were debt-free. According to Bill Yeargin, who has been sitting at the helm of Correct Craft as president and CEO since September 2006: "There are a lot of wonderful things that come from the heritage of Correct Craft and the Meloon family. Many of the Meloon family members are still very much a part of Correct Craft today – including 91-year-old patriarch and former chairman emeritus, Ralph Meloon (affectionately known as Mr. Ralph) and his son, Ken Meloon. We hold onto those timeless values and principles that have always defined Correct Craft. But to keep up with the changing times, we've put more aggressive forward-thinking in motion to ensure the future and solidarity of Correct Craft. What we're doing is preparing Correct Craft for the next 80 years"[41].

Another "Gospel"

"I marvel that you are turning away so soon from Him who called you in the grace of Christ, to different (another) gospel, which is not another; but there are some who trouble you and want to pervert the gospel of Christ. But even if we, or an angel from heaven, preach any other gospel o you than what we have preached to you, let him be accursed" Galatians 1: 6 -8

One should be correct to say that some of what some "evangelists" preach during crusades and "revival services" in developing countries could be classified as "another gospel". These preachers boldly make promises to their audience, such as the following:

143

"Those of you looking for husbands will find them, in the next one year"

"Each of you looking for the fruit of the womb will be blessed with a child within the next nine months"

"Those looking for a job, will each find a job, within the next one year".

"For you contractors, the Lord will bless you with overflowing wealth within one year".

The promises continue; listing what they know that people want to hear because that is what they are looking for. One of the effects of this is that any time such a crusade is advertised, the venues, and their nooks and crannies, and all roads leading to them, are over-crowded with people who have come in search of children, jobs, or any other such promised blessings!

One of the serious flaws of this type of preaching is that people get the wrong message that when they come to the Lord, all their problems, material, financial, physical, spiritual, etc., are solved immediately. This get-wealthy and all-problems-solved message is in sharp contrast with the reply of the Lord to some people who wanted to follow Him. He said: "....The foxes have holes, and the birds of the air have nests; but the Son of man hath not where to lay his head" (King James Version Mathew 8: 20). We are called as Christians to accept the Lord unconditionally as Saviour and Master. He has bought us with a price, which is His life given for us, which is worth more than silver and gold. It is not a commercial relationship that we enter into when we become Christians. The "pot" cannot tell the "potter" how to design it and for what purposes. The potter chooses to design the pot as He finds fit and for what use. In the same way, as Christians, we should consider and make ourselves available as vessels fit and prepared for the Master's use; and desist from dictating what we want from the Lord.

HE will mould us and use us as He finds fit in His design and the operation of His church to His glory. "Nevertheless, the solid foundation of God stands, having this seal: "The Lord knows those who are His," and, "Let everyone who names the name of Christ depart from iniquity". But in a great house there are not only vessels of gold and of silver, but also of wood and of clay, some for honour and some for dishonour. Therefore, if anyone cleanses himself from the latter, he will be a vessel for honour, sanctified, and useful for the Master, prepared for every good work" 2 Timothy 2: 19-21. It is equally the case that the Lord determines how to give out His physical and material blessings to His people, and all for His glory.

It is difficult to estimate and imagine the great harm done to the faith of gullible persons as and when they do not receive what they have been promised as the basis of their "conversion". Since unfortunately many people are prepared to believe anything in order to find solutions to physical, everyday problems. It is therefore essential that marketplace disciples have to disabuse their mind of the concept "of what is in it for me", as they serve the Lord. John the Baptist said: "He must increase, but I must decrease" John 3:30.

Marketplace disciples should not associate themselves with those peddling this dubious gospel.

God's faithfulness: The thoughts shared in the foregoing paragraph do not mean that the Lord does not bless His people and those who come to Him. For in Hebrews 11:6, we read: "But without faith it is impossible to please Him: for he who comes to God must believe that He is, and that He is a rewarder of them that diligently seek Him". Yes, the Lord rewards those who diligently seek Him and it is He and He alone who determines how and when He will reward them. We need to remember all the time that He has made us for His pleasure and not for our pleasure or glory. In Revelation 4:11, we read: "You are worthy, O Lord, to receive glory and honour and power: for you created all things. And by your will they exist and were created."

We now give the story of one of the men who was committed to serving the Lord and how the Lord blessed him richly. He was Henry Parsons Crowell. We have a lot to learn from his devotion in the service of the Lord and the successful applications of Biblical principles into his business operations.

Henry Parsons Crowell (founder of the Quaker Oats Company.) - **A Legacy of Integrity**

"If my life can always be lived so as to please Him in every way, I'll be supremely happy." —Henry Parsons Crowell [42].

He was born on January 27th, 1855 in Hartford, CT, of a Christian family. His father was a devout Christian who brought up his family in the fear of the Lord so much so that it was said that: "No meal was ever eaten in the Crowell home without first reading from the Scriptures. Thanksgiving and an entreaty for God's blessings on the home would follow[42]".

His father was not only concerned about their spiritual welfare but also with their physical and material welfare in the event that he died. His father died on November 24th 1864, the next day Henry went to his pastor who conducted his father burial and graveside services and spoke with him about his faith. After about an hour, Henry committed his life to the Lord. His father left him an inheritance of $27,000.00. Henry planned to go to Yale after his prep school but he became ill, contracting tuberculosis, the same disease that had killed his father.

In the spring of 1873, as he listened at the Second Presbyterian Church to "a fiery businessman turned evangelist," Dwight L. Moody, he was reportedly challenged by the words:

"The world has yet to see what God can do with and for and through and in a man who is fully and wholly consecrated to him. Will you be one of those men? Is your God worthy of such a commitment?"

Henry Crowell was reduced to tears, knowing that he had a knack for business, he said: "Maybe I can make money and help support men like D.L. Moody." He made the promise to the Lord that if He would bless him, he would support the work of the Gospel financially, including supporting men like D. L, Moody.

In spite of this commitment, his illness grew worse and he was bedridden most of the time. However, he did not give up rather continued in prayers and searching the Scriptures. In course of this, he became fascinated at the number of times that the number "seven" was used in the Scriptures. He personally claimed the promise in Job 5:19: "He shall deliver thee in six troubles: yea, in seven there shall be no evil touch thee." To keep this story short, he was healed in the seventh year following his claiming the promise.

As his health improved, so did his business. In the late 1870s, he made two very lucrative farm and real estate transactions. It started becoming apparent that he had the Midas touch – whatever business in which he got involved became lucrative. He was later approached by his uncle to buy a failing oats mill near Ravenna, OH, which was for sale.

Home work and business analysis: He took his time to study the business, doing his homework, questioning others in the business such as sales-men, other mill owners — anyone who knew anything about the business. At the age of 26, he bought the mill.

Prayers and marketing: He made the business a matter of daily prayer. He tried new ideas and innovations in marketing as follows:

1. He decided to package his products in attractive, colourful boxes for individual sales instead of dirty barrels that stay on the floor of general stores. Housewives found it attractive and the idea became an immediate success.

2. He formed a trust with other millers and experimented with joint-marketing efforts. This was more like our modern-day cooperatives. This was also a success.

3. His plan was to make Quaker a name on everyone's lips. He felt that advertising was effective only as it gave constant exposure to the product. He also pioneered the use of celebrity testimonials and endorsements to prove value.

4. He invented contests and prizes requiring the mailing in of a box top, did market testing and provided a heavy stream of sample products to give away at fairs, train stations, ball games and other places where crowds convened.

5. All these showed the power of his mind and the depth of his creativity. These were inventions that pre-dated his time and appeared as what we should have in contemporary advert agency.

Scriptural Basis: His use of the marketing techniques reveals that he practised scriptural principles in his efforts to grow his company. First, his desire to keep his product consistently before the public eye, via advertising methods, accords with the Biblical concept of repetition—"telling everything over and over again, a line at a time and in such simple words" Isaiah 28:10 (Living Bible).

Secondly, he knew the power of giving: "Give and it shall be given" (Luke 6:38). His confidence in his God, and his product, enabled him to give his product away and the returns were "supernatural."

Link with Rockefeller: Crowell and a partner, Frances Drury, started the Perfection Stove Company. In 1901, Drury had a deal with associates of John D. Rockefeller of Standard Oil. Rockfeller was to help them sell their stoves and this should help them sell kerosene, which was a by-product of their petroleum refining process. This proposal was right . Standard Oil had 3,000 salesmen who also sold the stove, Crowell agreed and sales immediately exploded beyond Crowell's wildest dreams. **Lesson:** Joint ventures often have mutual and exponential benefits for complementary products.

Successes in Civic Involvements: As a charter member of the Chicago Crime Commission, he and the Commission successfully pushed for local and state prosecutors to go after such vices that were present in Chicago, including illicit gambling, prostitution, and loansharkings.

Christian Giving: His dynamic Christian faith affected his business ventures, his civic involvement, and his generosity. During the latter part of Crowell's life, he was giving away close to 70 percent of his income. He supported many Christian endeavors, missionaries, churches, tract publication, prison ministries, and was sensitive to individual needs as well. He gave selflessly to widows, orphans, and those who had medical needs — even to young people seeking a higher education.

Moody Bible Institute: It is said that his support for the Moody Bible Institute was probably the most noteworthy aspect of his giving. It is also claimed that it could be true to say that "were it not for Crowell's support and management of Moody at a very crucial time in its history, the organization would not be here today". It was reported "that shortly after D.L Moody's death, the institution was suffering from a lack of funding—and direction. Crowell provided both. Once a week for 40 years, Henry Parsons Crowell took an entire day out of his very busy schedule and gave it to Moody Bible Institute by serving on the MBI Executive Committee. It was Crowell's gift of business that providentially rescued Moody Bible Institute"[42]. **Humility and Meekness:** It was reported that when the president of MBI wanted to name a new building after Crowell for his dedication to Moody, Crowell refused, because he had promised God early in his life that if He would allow him to make money to give to the gospel, he would keep his own name out of it. This was a classic demonstration of John 3:30, "That He must increase, but I must decrease." God had kept his promise and so did Crowell. It is evident that God honoured His servant's vow (Eccl. 5:5). As the scriptures teach us, God is not slack concerning His promises (2 Peter 3:9).

Death: On Monday, October 22nd, 1943, he boarded a train to return home from work, he took his seat on the train. As was his habit; opened his worn leather-bound New Testament to read but died as he read the word at the age of 88.

Belief and Support for Evangelical Christianity: As is normally the case, the activities of man perpetuate him and remain after he is gone. One of such was that in 1927, he formed a trust to perpetuate his desire to give to the work of God. He did not want his money to go to ministries that drifted from the fundamental truths of God's word. The Trust's website, www.crowellfoundation.org states:

"The establishment of the Crowell Trust with a purpose of 'encouraging and promoting the spread of Evangelical Christianity' has extended his mission years beyond his life on this earth, blessing hundreds of ministries each year and reaching to the far corners of the world".

Abiding Legacy: His life was a testimony not only to the power of God, but also to what God can do with any businessman "wholly consecrated to Him." We need to realise that it is the Lord who chooses who and how to give His blessings.

11

Some Contemporary Challenges Confronting Marketplace Disciples

ಕ

There are some challenges for the marketplace disciple both internally and externally. We shall start with internal challenges to discuss each of them.

Internal Challenges

The internal challenges come from his home, from his people. The Christian is challenged over money; he is compared with his colleagues. He is informed that some of his colleagues have built mansions but he has none. Some of his mates have cars but he is still using the one that he bought some years ago. Some of his mates have done a lot of good things for their people but he has not done much. The comparisons are made without any consideration of how his mates make their money or obtain their wealth. It is this type of inordinate pressure that the Christian faces among his people. Whilst it is in order to make progress and for his people to be concerned about his general welfare and progress in his career, the comparisons with his peers, as a yardstick to gauge progress, is unhelpful.

It is sad that in some churches sometimes undue recognition, praises, deference and honour are accorded to Christian professionals, entrepreneurs, and workers, etc., who are considered by their local churches to be wealthy and / or highly placed at their places of work. Some of these Christians tend to bask in such airs and try to nurture such a relationship that gives them ill-advised and unhelpful importance and "glory". The author has observed this failing in both Christians and churches in developing and developed countries. This is contrary to the Scriptures but it happens. These experiences constitute pressures. The mature Christian realises that he will do his level best at his job and earn money legitimately. He can and will do what he knows the Lord will approve of. He will not seek to make money at all costs in order to show his people that he has "arrived". It is the attitude of making money at all costs that makes the individual business person, who aspires to be a marketplace disciple, unfaithful to the Lord and to the business undertaking that he has made to his customers, including Christian brothers, on the use of fund. The mature Christian knows that such considerations are not compatible with being a light unto others as the Lord requires him to be. The Christian living faithfully will always pass the Mammon test as discussed earlier in this book.

Failure to see themselves as God's Disciples in the Marketplace

Again, Christians in the marketplace hardly recognize them-selves as marketplace disciples. They have not seen their careers as a holy calling and have not understood God's redemptive plan as applicable through their work and calling. Consequently, some often resign themselves as "financiers" of God's work instead of being a major catalyst for transformation of their workplaces and cities.

Moreover, some do not recognise that the Lord Jesus Christ is also Master of their vocations. That they need to do all things to please Him and not just their bosses or even their pastors.

External Challenges

External Challenges come from outside, at the place of work, in the city, nationally or internationally. This subject is also discussed later in this book under Money, Sex, and Power. However, it is rel-evant to suggest that there are also external religious organisations that are interested in causing confusion in countries in their unbridled ambition to foist Islam on developing countries. It is claimed that a lot of the riots that took place in recent times from 2007 – 2009, and even earlier, in the Northern states of Nigeria, for example, were planned from outside the country.

The Christian disciple in the marketplace should be watchful. "Watch and pray", as we are enjoined to do because the forces arraigned against the believer are desperate and care little about human lives and businesses which people have worked hard to build over the years. Some of the forces even claim that they want to erase all the vestiges and contributions of Western civilisation. However, we cannot discuss this subject further in this book as it could divert us from our subject.

12

Foundation for Success in the Marketplace Discipleship

ॐ

In view of the failures and challenges discussed in the foregoing chapters, it is relevant to suggest that each Christian should have the correct foundation on which they can build for success as a marketplace disciple. These include the following:

- Acceptance of the Lord Jesus Christ as Saviour and Lord
- Personal walk with the Lord with daily personal devotion and Bible studies
- Membership of a Gospel-preaching church
- Personal involvement in church fellowship and professional fellowship in the marketplace.
- Diligence in walking in holiness in all aspects of life, both public and private.

We shall discuss each of these suggestions. In addition, we shall take a look at the biographies of more Christians who had served the Lord in the marketplace and try to learn from their lives.

Acceptance of the Lord Jesus Christ as Saviour and Lord

One of the difficulties of building disciples among Christians in developing countries is the absence of true conversion among some of the church members. As discussed in the earlier sections, some claim conversion in the hope of material blessings such as finding a spouse, giving birth to a long-sought-for child, finding a new job, winning a lucrative contract, etc. As a result, many of such church members are not really committed to the Lord and have not experienced the new birth.

Some others claim to be Christians because their parents have been Christians and since they have been brought up in Christian homes, they say they are Christians. Again, they do not know the Lord and have no personal relationship with Him.

The starting point for each of us is to be sure that we are in the faith. Each individual who aspires to be used by the Lord should ask themselves: Am I born again? Do I know Jesus Christ as Lord and Master? The individual should consider and affirm the following points:

1. I am a sinner, I cannot relate to God or be right with Him on my own as my sins separate me from Him. Romans 3:23, Isaiah 59:1-2, Psalm 66: 18

2. I need to confess my sins and accept that I cannot do anything on my own to be right with Him without His help. John 1: 12, 3: 36b, Romans 1: 16

3. I have to accept that God realised that a man cannot save himself that is why He sent His Son into the world to die for the sins of every person who believes in Him. John 3: 16 – 18, Acts 4: 12, Romans 3:24-26, Romans 5: 8, Ephesians 2: 8-10

4. Having repented of my sins, especially the main sin of running my life, I now accept that Jesus Christ died to pay for my sins. When He hanged on the cross, he paid for my sins once and for all time. Romans 10: 9-10, Romans 4: 24 -25

5. I believe that He died and rose again and now accept Him as Saviour and Lord. Romans 8: 1-4, 14- 16

6. I accept Him as Saviour because He died on the cross and rose again to pay for my sins. He did for me what I cannot do for myself; indeed, what no other person can do for me. I accept Him as Lord because I have dedicated and committed my life to living for Him, to please and obey Him by entering into a personal relationship with Him. A relationship in which He guides me continually, daily, through the Holy Spirit such that I am His sheep and He is the Good Shepherd. He says: "My sheep hear my voice, and I know them, and they follow me. And I give unto them eternal life, and they shall never perish, neither shall any man pluck them out of my hand." John 10: 27 -28.

A relationship that is eternal such that nothing, no powers, not even death, can separate me from the Lord, Romans 8: 31- 39

7. As a Christian, I need to realise that my relationship is with the Lord and my commitment is unto Him and not to a church or to a pastor or to a priest. This is important because my decision to obey and live for Him is not determined by my geographical location, or church, or who is around me or with me. Whether I am alone in a desert or in the sea or in a hole or in a plane, in my native country or in a foreign country, wherever; the Lord sees me and He knows what I am doing each minute of my life. He knows whether I am really living for Him or not, I cannot hide away from Him. David wrote: "Where can I go from your Spirit? Or where can I flee from your presence? If I ascend into heaven, You are there; if I make my bed in hell, behold You are there. If I take the wings of the morning. And dwell in the uttermost parts of the sea. Even there Your hand shall lead me, and Your right hand shall hold me. If I say, "Surely the darkness shall fall on me." Even the night shall be light about me: indeed, the darkness shall not hide from You. But the night shines as day; the darkness and the light are both alike to You." Psalm 139:7-12.

8. "For the eyes of the Lord run to and fro throughout the whole earth, to show Himself strong on behalf of those whose heart is loyal to Him" 2nd Chronicles 16:9a. The fact that the Lord sees me all the time, knows the thoughts in my heart, and even every

imagination of my mind, underlines the futility and foolishness of pretending to be a Christian. For if I am a hypocrite, He knows it and I am deceiving no other person by myself. For if I am living right and walking with Him, He knows it and I really do not need to impress anyone with that fact because I should be living unto Him. For He has made each of us, including me for His pleasure, Revelation 4:11.

In the same vein, the fact that the Lord sees me all the time gives me the confidence similar to that of a child who knows that he is being watched and protected all the time by his father. The Lord knows that I am determined and committed to living for Him, and says to me and any other Christian: "......For you are the temple of the living God; as God has said: "I will dwell in them, and walk among them, I will be their God, and they shall be My people" 2 Cor.6:16b. We need to pause to appreciate the enormity of this promise. The fact that the God who spoke the world into existence, the Almighty God, the Omnipotent God, the Omniscient God, the All-wise God, is my Father, is a wonderful truth which each of us needs the light of the Spirit of God to help us comprehend.

Personal walk with the Lord through daily personal devotion and Bible studies

The efficacy of the personal relationship with the Lord is the confidence and conviction that I know the Lord, and the Spirit testifies to me that I am a child of God. "For as many as are led by the Spirit of God, these are the sons of God. For you did not receive the spirit of bondage again to fear; but you received the Spirit of adoption, by whom we cry, "Aba Father". The Spirit Himself bears witness with our spirit, that we are children of God", Romans 8: 14-16. The Christian lives daily in the consciousness that he has a heavenly Father who cares and is interested in him. In all he does, he seeks to please Him. This is why the Christian can take a stand for the Lord even when all others with him are refusing to accept what is correct. He knows that he has to walk with the Lord and with time, he will come to understand and appreciate that the walk with the Lord is the best experience an individual can have while here on earth.

Testimonies

1. A young Christian told his friends of his conversion: There was a young man who came to the Lord as a student in 1970 at the Federal School of Science, Lagos, Nigeria. One day, shortly after his conversion, he sat with his friends eating in the School dinning hall, and they started an unhelpful joke. He told them that he was not interested in the joke because he had become a Christian. They laughed at him, telling him that they could see members of the Christian Union all about on the campus, but for him, he had been one of them. He agreed that he had been one of them but explained to them that he had been converted and born again. They still laughed at him, telling him that time would tell. In fairness to him, they stopped the unhelpful joke. To the Lord be the glory that the young man stood firmly in his walk with the Lord. With time, his former colleagues saw that he was serious and never extended any such jokes to him again.

2. Alone in his hotel room: A young engineer assumed duties in a government electricity supply company, National Electric Power Authority, NEPA, and he was checked in to live in a top hotel in Benin City, now a capital city of one of the states in Nigeria. As he lay on his bed to rest at the end of the day, he tried the various switches in his room. As he turned on one of them, the music in the hotel bar started playing in his room. He carefully switched it off, saying this is not for me. There were other options to misbehave in a place that he was not known. Yes, no one knew him but he knew that the Lord was with him and knew everything he was doing, including the thoughts of his heart. "...and holiness, without which no one will see the Lord", Hebrews 12:14.

Prayer: "Pray without ceasing" (1Thessolians 5:17)

"Watch and pray..." Matthew 26:41.

"Be anxious for nothing, but in everything by prayer and sup-plications with thanksgiving, let your requests be made known to God" (Philippians 4:6).

On some occasions, the Lord Jesus Christ, who was God even here on earth, prayed all night. Other times, He left early to stay alone to pray. Many times, the author wonders that he does not pray as often and as much as he should if He, the Lord, could invest so much time in prayers. A personal walk with the Lord calls for prayers all the time. Apart from the daily devotional prayers in the mornings and evenings, the Christian continues in prayers all the time, several times a day. Praying as he goes to work, praying as he starts his day, praying as he is trying to solve a problem, praying in thanksgiving for answered prayers, praying at the end of the work day, praying before and after eating, praying as he faces a challenge or a tricky situation, praying in confession for wrong thoughts, wrong and ill-thought-out statements, wrong actions, and when he finds himself convicted by the Holy Spirit, etc. It is not the case that one can list all the times that prayers should be said but as the Christian walks with the Lord, he will appreciate the need to pray without ceasing as the Lord directs in His word, 1 Thessalonians 5:17.

Bible Studies: Daily Bible reading is essential for an effective walk with the Lord. The Spirit of God guides the Christian and interprets the word of God to him as he reads it daily. The walk with the Lord is as led by the Lord through His word so that the Christian is not just doing what he finds convenient; living just in his comfort zone, but he should live in obedience to the Lord as He directs in His word. This is why the Christian should read the word daily as commanded in the following passages: "This book of the law shall not depart from your mouth, but you will meditate in it day and night, that you may observe to do according to all that is written in it. For then you will make your way prosperous, and then you will have good success", Joshua 1: 8.

"How can a young man cleanse his way? By taking heed according to Your words" (Psalm 119: 9).

"Your word is a lamp to my feet and a light to my path" (Psalm 119 : 105).

"If you love Me, keep My commandments" (John 14:15).

"Be diligent to present yourself approved to God, a worker who does not need to be ashamed, rightly dividing the word of truth" (2Timothy 2:15).

There are many other Bible passages that underline the importance of daily Bible study for every individual Christian. We cannot remain steadfast and firmly rooted in the faith if we do not study the word of God every day. There are some helpful Bible study and personal devotional booklets which the Christian should find helpful. Some of these are produced by the Scripture Union. An example is "Encounter with God". It is one of the devotional series written quarterly. The booklet contains Bible passages to be read each day. The passages are discussed and the messages are interpreted in the light of contemporary events. In other words, the passage is not just left in the context of the Lord's dealing with the Israelites, for example, but are lifted to the context of the present day with its interpretation based on current national or international events as necessary.

It should be proper to submit that any Christian who is not prepared to read the Bible daily is not yet prepared to walk with the Lord. Strictly speaking, we shall be living in disobedience if we fail to study the Bible daily as commanded in Joshua 1:8.

Membership of a Gospel-preaching Church

We have made the point that the Christian is in a personal relationship with the Lord such that the commitment is to the Lord. This does not mean that he floats about or becomes a freelancer. The Bible does not recognise any such individual as a freelance Christian. No, the Christian has to belong to a gospel-preaching church. As the Christian studies the Bible, he will discover that every believer belonged to a group of believers. Even the Lord Jesus Christ, as God and man, also had His disciples and they worshipped in the synagogues. We are commanded not to forsake the assembly of believers, Hebrews 10: 25.

The Christian church is not a social gathering but a meeting of believers. It is a meeting of everyone who trusts the Lord Jesus Christ as Saviour and Lord. It is a meeting of people who are prepared to obey the Lord, and encourage one another to do the same. It is a meeting that is not determined by nationality, race, colour, status, etc. We are all members of one body, the body of Christ who by His death and resurrection paid for the sins of everyone who believes in Him and has united all believers in Him as members of the family of God. "But now in Christ Jesus you who were once far off have been brought near by the blood of Christ. For He Himself is our peace, who has made both one, and has broken down the middle wall of separation, having abolished in His flesh the enmity, that is the law of commandments contained in ordinances, so as to create in Himself one new man from the two, thus making peace, and that he might reconcile them both to God in one body through the cross, thereby putting to death the enmity. And He came and preached peace to you who were afar off and those who were near. For through Him we both have access by one Spirit to the Father. Now therefore, you are no longer strangers and foreigners, but fellow citizens with the saints and members of the household of God, having been built on the foundation of the apostles and prophets, Jesus Christ being the chief cornerstone." Ephesians 2: 13-20. Christian, irrespective of who you are or where you are from, you are as welcome to any Christian fellowship as any other Christian. It is a membership that has its right and responsibilities. Each Christian should attend fellowship meetings both at the weekend and during weekdays as organised by his church and make available his talents and gifts for the service of the Lord.

Personal Involvement in Church Fellowship and Professional Fellowship in the Marketplace.

The admonition not to forsake the assembly of believers, which we stated in the foregoing paragraph, is one that underscores the importance of fellowship for the Christian. It does not just command us to attend church service alone but also to attend fellowship meetings. It is such an important activity in the life of the Christian that there is a clear-cut command that we should join other believers in fellowship and not to forsake it.

Sometimes when one discusses with some people, they are quick to point out the faults in churches and their leadership to justify their failure to attend church service. It is perhaps a case of trying to find excuses for not belonging to a church and being active in it. It is equally instructive that the Lord knew the weaknesses, hypocrisies and shortcomings of the leaders of the synagogues and even denounced them. Yet He, the Perfect One, worshipped with them and did not avoid them.

"Iron sharpens iron" Proverbs 27:17. As iron sharpens iron, so a man sharpens the countenance of his friend.

"Though one may be overpowered by another, two can withstand him. And a threefold cord is not quickly broken" Ecclesiastes 4:12

The passages quoted above underline the necessity of fellowship and it should not be restricted to the church only but also extended to the workplace. In our contemporary societies, Christian professionals are finding themselves constrained by some legislations and laws. These tend to limit the practice of their faith at work. While individual Christians can discuss such experiences at their church fellowship meetings where prayers can be said for them, it is certainly the case that most people at the fellowship have no knowledge of what is being discussed and therefore may not fully appreciate the problems. This is where a fellowship of like professionals is necessary. A national fellowship of Christian lawyers, a fellowship of Christian doctors, a fellowship of Christian businessmen, a fellowship of Christian engineers, etc., could be more effective since their fellow professionals may discuss national legislations and practices that are hampering the practice of their faith in the marketplace. Each of these groups of professionals can effectively discuss such problems and decide on the way to handle the situation. If they need to make a formal complaint to the government they can do so with more impact and positive outcome than if an individual does so. If they do not pursue that option, they may agree on how to make progress in spite of the problems.

Fellowship also provides the opportunity for the Christian to use his talents to serve the group. Also the Christian gains from the service of other Christians who use their knowledge and gifts in the service of the group. While this happens often in Christian fellowship groups, it does not happen as extensively and widely as it should in most Christian professional groups. In such groups, especially in developing countries, the emphasis is mostly on spiritual issues, much is not discussed about the individual's professional career. This is unhelpful and we short-change ourselves by not using all our God given resources, whether spiritual or professional in "washing the feet of one another". It should be helpful therefore, if within a Christian professional group we discuss our career experiences, professional problems and successes so that others can learn from one another. We should learn to counsel Christian professionals with technical problems even as we counsel Christians when they have spiritual problems.

We should also be helpful to young Christian professionals who are new in the profession by advising them on the challenges and prospects before them. We could also guide them on how to circumvent some of the inevitable problems with which they will be confronted as they make progress in their professions in the marketplace.

13

Temptations of the Marketplace

࢙

P ower, money and sex are said to be the three main sources of temptations to the disciple and other players in the marketplace. Power is wielded by people in authority. Politicians, law officers, police officers, and employers wield power at different levels and with a lot of influence on society. The Christian is called to a vocation where he can serve the Lord as he discharges his daily responsibilities. Whether he is in a position to wield power or not is not really important as long as he is law-abiding and most importantly, walking everyday in the fear of God. He should have no fear for the Lord promises not to leave him or forsake him. He is guaranteed security in the Lord. Money is important and the medium of transactions in the marketplace. The Christian is warned against the love of money. Practically, this means that the individual should perform useful service to his society and earn money legitimately as he discharges such services. It should not be money at all costs, irrespective of how it is obtained.

It is also relevant to submit that the money the Christians earns should not only be for his personal use only. The necessity for contributions to the Lord's work is shown by the following two short real-life experiences.

As an engineer in a steel company in Nigeria, a Christian brother was a member of a church building committee. The committee had the task of raising fund for their church building as the federal government required them to vacate the school building where they were worshipping. The committee members went to as many Christian businessmen and wealthy professionals as they could within the country in search of money. It was sad that as they went to some of these benefactors, a number of them complained that they were being literally harassed by many Christian organisations asking for donations. The dire need for Christians who could give for the Lord's work was clearly underlined by the experiences narrated by the committee members.

The same engineer attended a prayer meeting in one of the churches in the UK and was surprised at the response he received when money was being discussed. He was made to feel that it was not proper for Christians to be praying for financial blessings. The argument was that the disciples of the Lord Jesus Christ were not wealthy, we should not pray for wealth.

When the same brother was in Ireland many years earlier as a young engineer, he had another experience. As they discussed door-to-door witnessing and he challenged other brethren on the necessity to get involved. An older Christian brother in the group thanked him

172

for his contribution, then gave this admonition. Brother, please tell your fellow brethren in Nigeria to try to contribute for the upkeep of their churches because the brethren in Ireland have been contributing for the upkeep of a Christian denomination in southern Nigeria. He mentioned the name of the denomination which was familiar to the brother.

Christians in developing countries need to support their churches and not depend on the Southern Baptist Church of the US or Baptist Churches in Ireland or any external organisation to pay their pastors and finance operations in their churches. The idea of depending on unbelievers to finance our programmes is certainly unacceptable. Corruption is one of the evils that is destroying our society as people embezzle money, enrich themselves by stealing public fund. We condemn and decry their activities. How then can we turn around and take money from them to fund our programmes? What we shall show to such people is love, urging them to repent of their sins and come to the Lord for salvation. Paul in his missionary journeys depended on the Lord and his own efforts. He wrote: "I coveted no one's silver or gold or apparel. Yes, you know that these hands have provided for my necessities, and for those who were with me. I have shown you in every way, by labouring like this, that you must support the weak. And remember the words of the Lord Jesus, that He said, "It is more blessed to give than to receive" Acts. 20:33-35. Again in Acts 16: 15, Lydia, a Christian convert pleaded with Paul and his team to use her accommodation.

Also, Christians need to cater for the financial needs of their immediate families. These family members do not receive any help from the government or any other sources. They also need to help needy Christian brethren as much as possible. In most of the countries, there is no social welfare or income support for people in want; such people have to be supported by their relatives or members of the church or live in abject poverty with its consequences.

The Christian should work hard to earn legitimate incomes that honour the Lord to meet all the above needs. In developed countries, some professionals do two jobs at a time without infringing on any employer's time. One could be their full time job and the other a part time job. In spite of all these, the Christian should attend his fellowship meetings regularly both at the weekend and during the week. All told, the Christian should seek to honour the Lord with all his skills and energy even with his money. The money he earns is to be used for the glory of God in solving problems around him both in and out of the church.

We consider a brief biography of a Christian businessman who took time to study biblical teachings on money. He is Larry Burkett.

Larry Burkett

He was born in 1939 in Winter park, FL, and was the fifth of eight children. His father was an electrician and struggled to make ends meet such that Larry experienced poverty during his childhood[43].

After his high school education, he joined the Air Force and later Strategic Air Command, working as an electrical engineer. He also earned degrees in Finance and Marketing. When he left the Air Force, he worked as an electrical-engineer at General Electric and also served as vice president at Testline, an electronics firm.

He became a Christian when he was vice president, this was after his wife was led to the Lord. He joined a church and became active in a Bible study class for businessmen. Having been told by one of the brethren in the Bible study that God had little interest in the financial lives of Christians. This challenged him to study his Bible and as a result discovered 700 verses in Scripture that deal with money and finances.

In 1973, he worked with Campus Crusade for Christ in their deferred-giving and estate planning department. In 1976 he started Christian Financial Concepts (CFC), a ministry that sought to teach biblically based financial concepts to other believers. He discovered that most Christians with whom he interacted had little idea about how to balance their budget or what the Bible says about debt.

His knowledge grew on the subject and his willingness to discuss in a down-to-earth way on personal finance gave him the reputation of an "expert" on the subject. His ministry grew so much over the next 15 years that in 2000, CFC merged with Howard Dayton and Crown Financial Ministries, where until his death in 2003 he served as the chairman of the board of directors.

His Contributions

He published more than 70 books, sales of which reportedly exceed 11 million copies. He had four radio programs which were: "Money Matters," "How to Manage Your Money," "MoneyWatch," and "A Money Minute." These were broadcast nationally on over 1,000 radio outlets. By his writings and broadcast, he showed himself as a great example of a Christian businessman using his talents for the glory of God. He also focused his energy on breaking down the barriers between the sacred and the "secular". He was also a pioneer in the Marketplace Movement. He invested a lot of efforts to educate Christians across the globe on what the Bible says about personal and small business finances, he thus made the church far richer because of it.

The third source of temptation is sex. Unfortunately, the taboo that illicit sex used to have is being eroded with time. The argument that it is an affair between consenting adults appears to lend it the legitimacy that it should not have. Irrespective of how society presents and dresses up the act, it is a sin. The Christian should not only run away from a relationship that can lead to it but should also avoid entertaining such thoughts in their mind. It is certainly foolhardy to take chances with a situation that could lead to such an illegal encounter. Samson with all his strength was humiliated because he allowed himself to lie on the laps of a strange woman. King Solomon was the wisest of men, yet he lost his relationship with God because of his many marriages with beautiful heathen princesses. There will always be attractive beautiful ladies and handsome men. However, it will be foolhardy for the Christian to gaze at them and become very preoccupied with lust as to lose their discipline.

It appears that there is so much in the sexual act that we humans still do not understand even though we treat it casually to our detriment. For one thing the Lord commands against illicit sex. The worship of Baal and other idols involved sex with temple prostitutes or priestess while so-called temple priest had sex with women who had come to worship. In other words, illicit sex features in the worship of some idols. The expression: "sanctity of sex" appears to carry more message than we seem to understand now.

On a practical level, it does not make sense that one endangers one's relationship with the Lord, and with one's spouse because of an act that could last for thirty minutes. A transient "pleasure" of thirty minutes that throws down the drain all the values that one has built up in one's life. It does not make sense. The right attitude is to flee as the wise Joseph did before his master's wife and even ended up being banged into prison on false charges. Yes better in prison on false charges to the glory of God who at His own time took him out and made him the prime minister of Egypt. It makes sense to fear God and live for Him when no other person knows what is happening. The Lord knows and will vindicate the Christian at His own time.

Man in Christ is the disciple required for the marketplace.

A brother gave the testimony that the walk with the Lord makes a person better than the laws of any country can ever produce. His experience as he travels from one part of the world to the other as an international businessman is that he goes about without fear. Rather he travels with confidence as he passes through customs and immigration officers at the different international airports in the knowledge that he will not do anything illegal and nothing illegal will be found around him or associated with him. The discipline the Lord has given him and continues to give him daily is such that he is more disciplined than the standards set by international laws. The reason for the confidence is that the personal walk with the Lord makes the individual Christian live in the grace of God which teaches them to deny ungodliness and worldly lusts, and live soberly, righteously, and godly, in this present world. In stead of living to copy the behaviours of their colleagues in the marketplace and using them as standards, the Christian disciple is kept by the grace of God and challenged to keep looking for that blessed hope, and glorious appearing of the great God and our Saviour Jesus Christ. For the purpose of our salvation is that we have been redeem from all iniquity, and purified to become a peculiar people, zealous of good works. This is the type of person that the Lord will use in the healing of our nations. In all these, the Christian should know that on his own, he will fall but his daily walk should be in the Lord because without Him, we can do nothing, John 15: 5.

14

Standing Firmly as a Marketplace Disciple and Prerequisites for City Transformation

ॐ

Following a foundation built on genuine conversion and continual walk with the Lord, it is correct to suggest that standing firmly continually in faith is a prerequisite for success in view of the ever present temptations in the marketplace . It is also relevant to advise that being active alone in the church without being in active walk with the Lord is not getting it right. St. Paul admonishes: "Therefore, let him who thinks he stands take heed lest he fall" 1 Corinthians 10: 12. He also says: "But I discipline my body and bring it under subjection, lest, when I have preached to others, I myself should become disqualified" 1 Corinthians 9:27. This passage and others emphasize that Christians need to live a life of prayer and discipline, as Paul also says: "No one engaged in warfare entangles himself with the affairs of this life, that he may please him who enlisted him as a soldier" 2Timothy 2:4.

In addition to devotional practices discussed earlier for effective Christian living, we suggest other key ingredients for effectiveness as marketplace or front-line Christian "soldiers" involved in the transformation of cities. They include:

1. Prayer
2. Humility
3. Unity
4. Knowledge of God's ways

Prayer

In every city where transformation or revival has taken place believers have had to come together to pray for their city. Prayer changes the spiritual climate of a city. "When God intends great mercy for His people, the first thing He does is to set them a – praying"[44]. *"If My people, who are called by My name will humble themselves and pray and seek My face and turn from their wicked ways, then will I hear from heaven and will forgive their sin and will heal their land"* 2 Chronicles 7:14. There are some key topics which are suggested to be the focus of our prayers for changes to occur in our cities.

Prayer for Leaders - 7 Key Areas

We must identify and pray for city leaders in 7 domains and these general categories.

- Churches – all churches and denominations in the city

- Law and order
- Business
- Politics and governance
- Education
- Medical, science and technology
- Media and Entertainment

In praying for business, there is the classic story of Dr. George Washington Carver which testifies to the effectiveness of prayers in science and business. Yes, prayer has a place for transformation of cities, in science and technology, and for the Christian professionals in their secular work in the marketplace.

Inventions in Agriculture Through Prayer – George Washington Carver

It is said of George Washington Carver that he got up early in the morning each day to walk alone and pray. He asked God how he was to spend his day and what He wanted to teach him that day. Carver grew up at the close of the Civil War in a one-room shanty on the home of Moses Carver, the man who owned his mother[45]. The Ku Klux Klan had abducted him and his mother, selling them to new owners. He was later found and returned to his owner, but his mother was never seen again.

Carver grew up at the height of racial discrimination, yet he had overcome all these obstacles to become one of the most influential men in the history of the United States. He made many discoveries with the use of peanuts and sweet potatoes.

George Washington Carver understood that his calling from God was his work. He lost his mother to slave traders. If there was ever a man who deserved to be a victim of his circumstances, it was he. But God had a plan for his life. He came to faith in Christ as a young boy and although God gave Carver an inventive mind, he had his education under great adversity. Eventually, Carver would become an inventor and have his own laboratory where he would spend time with God early in the morning. The southern agricultural economy was in a shambles after hundreds of years of planting cotton. The land was no longer fertile. Carver was seeking to provide an alternative crop for the farmers. However, on an occasion when he recommended farmers to plant peanuts and sweet potatoes instead of cotton, he experienced his greatest trial. The farmers lost even more money due to the lack of market for peanuts and sweet potatoes. Carver cried out to the Lord, "Mr. Creator, why did You make the peanut?" Many years later, he shared that God led him back to his lab and worked with him to discover some 300 marketable products from the peanut. Likewise, he made over 100 discoveries from the sweet potato. These new products created a demand for peanuts and sweet potatoes, and they were major contributors to rejuvenating the Southern economy.

As he made new discoveries, he never became successful monetarily, but he overcame great rejection during his lifetime for being black. He was offered six-figure income opportunities from Henry Ford, and he became friends with presidents of his day, yet he knew what God had called him to do. His epitaph read: He could have added fortune to fame, but caring for neither, he found happiness and honour in being helpful to the world [46]. Economists and agriculturalists agree that Carver contributed more than any other individual to rejuvenate the Southern economy.

The next section has been taken from the website of the University of Tuskegee where George Carver is described as a scientist extraordinaire.

- Dr. George W. Carver : Scientist Extraordinaire, Man of Faith, Educator and Humanitarian - A legend of Tuskegee University[47].

As a botany and agriculture teacher to the children of ex-slaves, Dr. George Washington Carver wanted to improve the lot of "the man farthest down," the poor, one-horse farmer at the mercy of the market and chained to land exhausted by cotton. Unlike other agricultural researchers of his time, Dr. Carver saw the need to devise practical farming methods for this kind of farmer. He wanted to coax them away from cotton to such soil-enhancing, protein-rich crops as soybeans and peanuts and to teach them self-sufficiency and conservation. Having succeeded in inventing how to use the crops, he went on to disseminate the information.

Dr. Carver achieved this through an innovative series of free, simply-written brochures that included information on crops, cultivation techniques, and recipes for nutritious meals. He also urged the farmers to submit samples of their soil and water for analysis and taught them livestock care and food preservation techniques.

In 1906, he designed the Jessup Wagon, a demonstration laboratory on wheels, which he believed to be his most significant contribution toward educating farmers. His practical and benevolent approach to science was based on a profound religious faith to which he attributed all his accomplishments. He always believed that faith and inquiry were not only compatible paths to knowledge, but that their interaction was essential if truth in all its manifold complexity was to be approximated.

Always modest about his success, he saw himself as a vehicle through which God, nature, and the natural bounty of the land could be better understood and appreciated for the good of all people. He took a holistic approach to knowledge, which embraced faith and inquiry in a unified quest for truth. Carver also believed that commitment to God is necessary if science and technology are to serve human needs rather than the egos of the powerful. His belief in service was a direct outgrowth and expression of his wedding of inquiry and commitment. One of his favourite sayings was:

"It is not the style of clothes one wears, neither the kind of automobile one drives, nor the amount of money one has in the bank, that counts. These mean nothing. It is simply service that measures success."

The website continues with this statement: "Our nation currently agonizes over questions about ethics and society in the wake of egregious moral abuses in our public and private lives. The life of Carver reminds us that such abuses will continue until we reunite ethical and technical reasoning in the context of a profound faith that holds all inquiry and action accountable. Accomplishing this in the midst of so much diversity will not be easy. We can, however, approximate it if we act on the belief in a common humanity, which binds us together despite our differences of race, nationality and culture, and a common destiny that can be secured only if science and technology seek to serve broad and deep societal needs".

Dr. George Carver attended the University of Tuskegee, in the next section on "humility" we shall also learn from the biography of Booker T. Washington how the Lord blessed him in his humility. He was the first teacher and first President of University of Tuskegee.

Humility

God uses men and women who recognize they need one another and do not seek glory for their work. This is the kind of leader God wishes to use even today. *"The humble He guides in justice. And the humble He teaches his way"* Psalm 25:9. *A man's pride will bring him low, But the humble in spirit will retain honour"* Proverbs 29:23. The Bible shows that Moses was the most humble man on earth. This is why God used him to deliver a people from slavery and bondage. *"Now the man Moses was a very humble, more than all men who were on the face of the earth"* Numbers 12:3.

At this point, it could be relevant to introduce a humble man that the Lord raised through Christian discipline and hard work from slavery and poverty to becoming one of the greatest business educators. He was from a humble background and when he became successful, he remained humble in spirit and tried to improve the lots of the poor, and this underlines his humility. He was Dr. Booker T. Washington.

A biography of Booker T. Washington (1856-1915)

"My life had its beginning in the midst of the most miserable, desolate, and discouraging surroundings", so wrote the great black educator Booker T. Washington on the first page of his autobiography, *Up From Slavery*.

He was born a slave on a Virginia farm in 1858 and reported that the formative years of his life consisted of nothing but hard labour and a home devoid of even the most basic comforts *and* "civilities" that most Christians take for granted. For example, he wrote: "I cannot remember a single instance during my childhood or early boyhood when our entire family sat down to the table together, and God's blessing was asked, and the family ate a meal in a civilized manner" [48].

In spite of this extreme poverty, Booker T. Washington grew up to become one of the most powerful and respected men in America in the early 20th Century. One of the habits that led to his success included the yearning to read. He wrote:

"From the time that I can remember having any thoughts about anything, I recall that I had an intense longing to learn to read. I determined, when quite a small child, that, if I accomplished nothing else in life, I would in some way get enough education to enable me to read common books and newspapers."

In spite of this desire, at the end of the American Civil War, his family ended up in West Virginia and he started work in a coal mine and not in a school. It was there that he heard about a school, the Hampton Normal and Agricultural Institute in Virginia, established especially for blacks. He immediately resolved to attend this school. He could not rid himself of the seemingly impossible notion that he could travel hundreds of miles to Hampton and be admitted. "I had no idea where it was,' he wrote, "or how many miles away, or how I was going to reach it; I remembered only that I was on fire constantly with one ambition, and that was to go to Hampton."

He determined to go to the school. He got as far as Richmond and spent a few days there sleeping under a plank sidewalk at night and loading a ship during the day to earn money to buy food. He arrived at Hampton Institute and the lady principal told him to sweep a room for her. He knew it was a test. He swept and dusted the room three times until not a speck of dirt remained. He was accepted into the school. He would work as the assistant janitor to pay for his room and board at the school. In spite of his heavy course load, he graduated with honours in just three years.

After graduation he returned to his hometown, Malden, and became a teacher at the first school he ever attended. In the day school he had a class of 80-90 students. He also taught night classes and two Sunday schools. He encouraged several of his students to attend Hampton Institute. He also sent his brother John and adopted brother James to the school.

General Armstrong, the principal at Hampton, invited Booker to return to the school as a teacher and a post-graduate student. He taught a night class for students who had to work during the day. He also taught a class of 75 Indian boys. He was being groomed to lead the growing school, but the Lord had other plans. Wilbur Foster, a former Confederate colonel, an Alabama legislator, introduced a bill in the Alabama legislature to establish a school for black teachers for benefit of former slaves and their children. The bill was passed and General Samuel C. Armstrong, the headmaster of Hampton Institute, was required to recommend a head for the new school in Tuskegee, Alabama. Without hesitation, he suggested Booker T. Washington. Booker was offered the position and he accepted it. Driven by his determination, Washington built Tuskegee Institute into a school of 107 buildings on 2,000 acres with over 1,500 students and more than 200 teachers and professors. One of his major contributions to mankind as an educator was his approach to higher education which makes his philosophy of education relevant for entrepreneurs to study. It consisted of an emphasis on the traditional academic courses and the requirement for students to learn industry and trade skills. For example, the students learned brick laying, forestry and timber skills, sewing, cooking, agriculture, etc. Every student was required to master at least two trades so that he or she would always be able to contribute to the industry and betterment of society and be self-supporting after graduation. His objectives at Tuskegee Institute included training students to become independent small businessmen, farmers, and teachers and not just salaried workers. Booker T. Washington was an eloquent speaker and used this skill for the benefit of Tuskegee Institute. The school continued to grow.

Political and Social Contributions

For decades, Booker T. Washington was the major African-American spokesman in the eyes of white America. He was a handsome man and a forceful speaker, and was skilled at politics. Powerful and influential in both the black and white communities, Washington was a confidential advisor to presidents. For years, presidential political appointments of African-Americans were cleared through him. He was funded by Andrew Carnegie and John D. Rockefeller, dined at the White House with Theodore Roosevelt and family, and was the guest of the Queen of England at Windsor Castle.

Although Washington was an accommodator, he spoke out against lynchings and worked to make "separate" facilities more "equal." Although he advised African-Americans to abide by segregation codes, he often travelled in private railroad cars and stayed in good hotels.

In 1895 he was invited to give a speech at an Exposition in Atlanta. In it he urged blacks and whites to work together. Afterwards Harvard University gave him an honorary degree.

Relationship with the Lord

He was a devoted Christian and ensured that morning and evening prayers were held every day in the school. A writer suggests that the life of Booker T. Washington should be a required study for every school child in America and indeed in the rest of the world. His legacy could be summed up in the fact that in spite of his humble beginnings as a slave and his "discouraging surroundings" he was later able to say, "It is at the bottom of life we must begin, and not at the top." Yet by dint of hard work, faith in God and the drive to succeed, he ended up at the top.

This is a lesson that every Christian in the marketplace should master. Our background should not be an excuse to continue in poverty and live in utter dependence on handouts and gifts from others. The Lord has shown through the life of a destitute slave named Booker T. Washington who was determined to trust Him, work hard with a vision for success, and succeeded to become one of the foremost educators that the world had seen. He was used by the Lord to make the world a better place for thousands of people who graduated from the school that he built. Today, the Tuskegee Institute opened on July 4, 1881, is the Tuskegee University, an American national, independent, and state-related institution of higher learning in the State of Alabama. It may be relevant to learn more about Booker T. Washington from the history of Tuskegee University which we also discussed when we studied about Dr. George Washington Carver.

History of Tuskegee University and Washington

Welcome to Tuskegee University- "the pride of the swift, growing south." It was founded in a one room shanty, near Butler Chapel AME Zion Church, thirty adults represented the first class - Dr. Booker T. Washington the first teacher. The founding date was July 4, 1881, authorized by House Bill 165.

The site contains these words: "We should give credit to George Campbell, a former slave owner, and Lewis Adams, a former slave, tinsmith and community leader, for their roles in the founding of the University. Adams had not had a day of formal education but could read and write. In addition to being a tinsmith, he was also a shoemaker and harness-maker. And he could well have been experienced in other trades".

The site introduces W. F. Foster, who was a candidate for re-election to the Alabama Senate. He approached Lewis Adams for the support of African-Americans in Macon County. What would Adams want, Foster asked, in exchange for the black vote. Adams could well have asked for money, instead, he wanted an educational institution - a school - for his people. Col. Foster carried out his promise and with the assistance of his colleague in the House of Representatives, Arthur L. Brooks, legislation was passed for the establishment of a "Negro Normal School in Tuskegee." A $2,000 appropriation, for teachers' salaries, was authorized by the legislation and a board of commissioners was formed. They sent word to Hampton Institute in Virginia looking for a teacher and Booker T. Washington was appointed as the first principal of the school from July 4, 1881, until his death in 1915. Tuskegee rose to national prominence under the leadership of its founder, Dr. Washington. During his tenure, institutional independence was gained in 1892, again through legislation, when Tuskegee Normal and Industrial Institute was granted authority to act independent of the state of Alabama.

Dr. Washington, a highly skilled organizer and fund-raiser, was counsel to American Presidents, a strong advocate of Negro business, and instrumental in the development of educational institutions throughout the South. He maintained a lifelong devotion to his institution and to his home - the South. Booker T. Washington, more than any other black man of his time, helped to elevate his people through education. Dr. Washington is buried on the campus of Tuskegee University near the University Chapel.

At the time of his death, there were 1,500 students, a $2 million endowment, 40 trades, (we would call them majors today), 100 fully-equipped buildings, and about 200 faculty. From 30 adult students in a one room shanty, we have today grown to more than 3,000 students on a campus (the main campus, farm and forest land) that includes some 5,000 acres and more than 70 buildings. Dedicated in 1922, the Booker T. Washington Monument, called "Lifting the Veil," stands at the centre of campus. The inscription at its base reads, "He lifted the veil of ignorance from his people and pointed the way to progress through education and industry." For Tuskegee, the process of unveiling is continuous and lifelong.

Unity

As has been stressed in this book, Unity is a core ingredient of city transformation. Jesus tells us in John 17: "I have given them the glory that you gave me, that they may be one as we are one: I in them and you in me. May they be brought to complete unity to let the world know that you sent me and have loved them even as you have loved me" John 17:22-23. Unity does not just happen. It is built when we roll up our sleeves and enter the battle of prayers together. Christians in the marketplace and the church must come together in unity to pray for the city.

There are two examples of persons of prayers who were used by the Lord in uniting His people to achieve much to His glory. We shall discuss briefly the lives of Nehemiah and James Hudson Taylor, drawing lessons for our own applications.

Nehemiah

Nehemiah, a man of prayers who walked with God, was a cupbearer or steward, a city builder, and later a governor of Judah who devoted his life to doing God's will. At the start of his career, he left the security and comfort of his job as the cupbearer to King Artaxerxes of Persia to return to Jerusalem in his determination to rebuild the walls of Jerusalem. Seventy years earlier, Zerubabel had rebuilt the temple, and thirteen years before Nehemiah's visit, Ezra had tried to lead a spiritual reawakening of the people. However, the walls of the city still lay broken down and Nehemiah knew no peace when he received a first hand report of the situation.

He had to pray to the Lord before taking the delicate step of seeking permission from the king to travel to Jerusalem. He remained fervent in prayers as he obtained all the relevant clearance papers and permission from respective officers that could give him the free hand to work with his people and the resources needed in his task of rebuilding the wall.

Still prayerful, he showed amazing leadership skills in uniting the people on the project in spite of the hostility of Sanballat and Tobiah from Samaria. It is to his credit that he displayed sterling statesmanship in leading the people to complete the task in a record time. In addition, the Lord used Nehemiah to cause spiritual revival among his people. His activities as a leader in Jerusalem provides some object lessons in effective leadership as given in a Bible footnote [49]. The note is modified and the message summarised as follows:

1. Establish a clearly defined goal or purpose
2. Continually evaluate the goal in the light of the word of God and His revealed will.

3. Be straightforward, honest and a person of integrity. Nehemiah made his purpose and needs clear. He spoke the truth even when it made it more difficult for him to achieve his goal.

4. Live above board, in spite of accusations that may be made against you falsely. Nehemiah faced false accusations even though he was a man of integrity.

5. Be prayerful and try to derive wisdom and guidance in your prayers and bible study. Nehemiah talked with God, sharing his thoughts, anxieties, feelings and dreams with Him. He walked with God, putting into action what he learned in his continuous talks with Him. Therefore in his endeavour to obey God, he solved almost impossible problems to the glory of God.

James Hudson Taylor 1832 - 1905

James Hudson Taylor, a man of faith and prayers, a dedicated and diligent servant of the Lord was the founder of the China Inland Mission. He was one of the greatest missionaries of all time and made great contributions to the evangelisation of China in the nineteenth century. It is reported that:

- When he arrived China, there were only 350 believers but at the time of his death there were over 175,000.

- When he arrived, there were only 80 missions but at his death, there were 3,800. The largest of these missions were from the China Inland Mission, the mission that he founded

As a man used by the Lord to do the Lord's job by uniting teams of the Lord's people, he not only did not have any denominational affiliation or backing for his ministry, but also his choice of missionaries was determined by their faith in the Lord. The missionaries were selected on their individual practice of the Christian faith but not on their narrow divisive denominational qualifications.

Early life and conversion

He became a Christian at the age of 17 and believed he had a missionary call to China. His father was a chemist but he decided to spend some time with his uncle a doctor in Hull to learn some basic skills in medicine which should help him in his mission. Later in life, he returned to London to complete his medical studies and still went back to China on his missionary work. He studied medicine and surgery because medical missionaries were greatly needed at the time in China.

After moving out of his uncle's home and living on his own, one evening he was requested to pray for the wife of an Irish labourer who was dying. It was reported that he found the lady weak not only because of child birth but also because of hunger. He was convinced that he should do more than pray. He reasoned that the Lord had sent him to the lady and if he could not do what he could do, how would he expect the Lord to answer his prayers. He then gave the lady's husband half a crown to go and buy food for her; this was the only money he had for his upkeep, (half a crown was 12.5 pence). The next day, the Lord provided half a sovereign to him through a gift from someone, (half a sovereign was 50 pence, four times what he gave out). This experience convinced him that the Lord would never fail those who trust Him, and this started his life of believing and trusting the Lord.

Highlights of His Work and His Personal Qualities

It may be instructive to examine selected events in his life which underline his faith in the Lord and his commitment to missionary work. Some of them are as follows:

1. **His Six Distinctive Qualities for Selecting Missionaries for the China Inland Mission**

   1. Missionaries were drawn from any denomination, provided they could sign a simple doctrinal declaration. He wanted most importantly candidates with the required spiritual qualities.

   2. They were to receive no guaranteed salary, but trusted the Lord to supply their needs. Income would be shared. No debts would be incurred.

   3. No appeals for funds were to be made. Taylor often reportedly said:"God's work carried on in God's way will never lack God's supply." The CIM worked on the same principles.

4. The work in China would be directed not by home commit-tees in England, or in the US etc., but by Hudson Taylor, himself and eventually other leaders in the field in China.

5. The organization would advance the gospel into China's interior ("where Christ had not been named"). The gospel's rapid spread led to Taylor's insistence that workers continue gospel-preaching trips throughout the provinces of China. Their example incited other missions to extensive evange-listic efforts.

6. The missionaries would wear Chinese clothes and worship in Chinese-styled buildings. They would not call on western powers for protection. To Taylor, enduring persecution was "ten thousand times better than writing to the Consul and get-ting him to appeal to the Viceroy." (Bays, 61)

It might be relevant to add that he had the foresight and was blessed with the wisdom to involve women on the mission field to be used in many different roles, particularly among the Chinese women. The women missionaries could often get where no male missionary could. Thus they were indispensable in furthering the work of the mission.

2. He was a man of faith and the Pioneer of "Faith Missions"

As a person, he lived by faith and his life demonstrated his faith as exemplified by the statement credited to him: "There is a living

God. He has spoken in His Word. He means what He says. And He is willing and able to perform what He has promised."

Hudson Taylor's founding of the China Inland Mission began the 'Faith Mission Movement'. As many as forty other faith mission boards were after founded along similar lines. Some of these include the Christian & Missionary Alliance (1887); the Evangelical Alliance Mission (1890), the Central American Mission (1890), the Sudan Interior Mission (1893), and the African Inland Mission (1895)

3. Fostered Unity and Harmony

He was non sectarian as his focus was on evangelism. During his various tours around the UK, US, Canada, etc., he appealed to believers in all denominations to support their own mission programs. In China he held together a diverse group of hundreds of workers from most major denominations such that CIM missionaries were a large and diverse group. Recruits came from all major denominations in Britain and other English-speaking countries, plus Germany, Switzerland and Scandinavia. Yet, when they arrived in China and worked under the umbrella of CIM, they were all part of the "large CIM family." Kane writes that: "That this large, international, heterogeneous group of active, strong-minded missionaries could achieve and maintain a high degree of harmony over a long period of time was a tribute to the wise, gentle, but forceful leadership of Hudson Taylor" [51].

4. Strong Determination and Hard Work

Taylor's success owed much to his determination and dedication to hard work. His prayer was matched by focused labour. His son wrote, "Hudson Taylor prayed about things as if everything depended upon the praying, but then he worked as if everything depended upon the work."

Taylor wrote a poem:

Who spoke of rest? There is rest above./ No rest on earth for me. On, on to do/ My Father's business. He, who sent me here,/ Appointed me my time on earth to bide,/ And set me all my work to do for Him,/ He will supply me with sufficient grace - / Grace to be doing, to be suffering / Not to be resting. There is rest above.

A Canadian doctor, Dr. De la Porte, observed Hudson Taylor. He wrote:"I have seen him come home at the close of the day footsore and weary, his face covered with blisters from the heat of the sun. He would throw himself down to rest in a state of utter exhaustion, and then get up again in a few hours to face the toil and hardship of another day. It was clear to me that he enjoyed the highest respect from the Chinese, and was doing a great deal of good among them" [51].

His example clearly gives the message that prayer is not an alternative to hard work and hard work does not preclude prayers. Prayers and hard work go hand in hand [52].

Thus far in this chapter, we have discussed three of the four key ingredients suggested for effectiveness as marketplace or frontline Christian "soldiers" involved in the transformation of cities. They are: Prayer, Humility, and Unity. We shall now discuss, Knowledge of God's Ways, the last of the suggested ingredients.

Knowledge of God's Ways

"My people perish because of lack of knowledge ..." Hosea 4:6. Irrespective of our zeal, we need to do everything in reverence to the Lord. We can learn from the experience of David in the initial failed attempt of returning the ark to the city. David wanted to bring the Ark of the Covenant into the city of Jerusalem. He was zealous for God and celebrated as he brought the Ark into the city. However, as the Ark was being carried into the city on a cart, Uzzah reached out to catch the Ark when they stumbled. He was stricken dead by God and David was devastated, 2 Sam 6:6-7.

This experience helps underline the need for unity and the complementary service that should exist between the sacred and the secular. The pastors will advise and direct on activities, services, and practices acceptable to the Lord based on the Word of God. The marketplace Christians will work using such advice, knowledge of the Word of God, and leading of the Holy Spirit to carry out activities to glorify the Lord as the two groups engage in prayers for effective witnessing.

David Oliver Love Work, Live Life! And discussion of some real-life contemporary cases [53]

An event called Love Work, Live Life! challenges the perception that 'secular' employment is 'second class'. "For too long we've mistakenly assumed that the only work God is interested in is Christian 'ministry'," says David Oliver, who presents the event. "But the majority of people in the Bible worked in 'secular' jobs – and God wanted them there!"

Love Work, Live Life is the ministry of international businessman, keynote speaker and church leader David Oliver. It is dedicated to seeing all God's people released to full time front line ministry in every sphere of life and work. Helping church members see their workplace as a primary calling in God. Working hard to break down the so called 'sacred secular' divide, Love Work, Live Life helps listeners go away empowered and inspired to make a life-long difference in their places of work.

Having taken events to over 60 towns and cities in the UK, David has been taking his message to US towns and cities. He believes every job, from an air hostess to a zookeeper (and anything in between), can be rewarding and fulfilling for Christians. In the following paragraphs, three people, from different workplaces, ask David about how to live for God in the daily challenges they face. We start with Maria.

Maria, a Primary School Teacher: She has been a primary school teacher for ten years. In her work she receives affirmation from other Christians. However, becoming a mum has left her 'feeling torn': "I find it difficult not working full time, as that would benefit the children I teach. But I also feel that, as a mum, I have a new priority." "How do you balance a job that affects other people's lives with being a committed parent?"

David has four children himself and had to find his own answers to this question. "Firstly, make sure that God has definitely called you to that particular job – and that both you and your spouse agree on this. Secondly, pray that God will help you find time to be together as a family. Then resolve to put your family before your career. Find times that you can routinely give to your kids, to your spouse and to yourself. Form your own family traditions – special times that each member of your family will remember and treasure for years to come. And ask people to pray for you and your family."

"How do I express my views as a Christian without forcing them on the children I teach, especially dealing with multi-faith issues where all religious beliefs are taught equally?"

"You have to be careful about what you do in your employer's time," advises David. "You're not paid to evangelise. So try to live your beliefs in the way that you work. If you look at the story of Daniel, the folks around him would have said from his devotion to duty and worship of his God: 'Don't tell me what you know until you show me what you can do'. In your situation it may help to say something like: 'As you know, all religions are taught here, and in line with that I'm going to tell you what I believe.' But again, people need to see it in your actions first." The second person is Ruth.

Ruth, a business entrepreneur: She runs her own business, Diamond Home Improvements, selling double glazing. She says many of her customers value doing business with a Christian: "People find it refreshing to find an honest person in what is seen as a dishonest business." Ruth also has a growing career in radio broadcasting, moving on from local Christian radio to BBC Radio 4. "As a sales person, how much pressure should I apply to close the sale?"

As David earns his living through sales, this question is one he has asked himself. "There are two basic principles to selling: motivation and manipulation. If you motivate someone to make a good decision, and encourage them to do what they want or need to do, then that is a godly and right way to act. If you're manipulating someone to do what isn't in their best interests, then that isn't godly and is ultimately unsustainable. You won't get repeat business from acting in an underhand way. But people do procrastinate. Sometimes they have to be persuaded to do the right thing!"

"In terms of making money, how much personal ambition should you have?"

David has a strong view on this: "It comes down to your definition of success. For me, 'success' isn't defined by possessions or money; it's obedience to God. Most people would expect a salesperson to make money and there's nothing wrong with being fruitful. But making money shouldn't be your core value – profit should be the fruit, not the root."

The third person is Rhys.

Rhys, a grocery storeman: He works in the grocery department of a supermarket. Despite being known as one of the few Christians in the 300-strong team, and being nicknamed 'Monk' by the other lads, he says: "They respect me for being different."

"How do you deal with awkward customers who are blaming you for something that's gone wrong, but isn't your fault?"

David believes this revolves around what he calls the 'bottom line' when it comes to being a Christian at work. "Loving your neighbour as yourself means putting yourself in their position. Work out what you would want done if you were making the complaint, and try to do that. It's not easy when someone is being obnoxious, but try to listen and empathise, and then propose a solution. The thing that really annoys people is when companies refuse to take responsibility. If you can take responsibility, not for the original problem, but for finding a solution, then they will often be grateful."

"Many of the people I work with talk about relationships all the time. How do I explain to a non-Christian work colleague my views on relationships if they want something more than friendship?"

"Asking this question shows real integrity," says David. "It's the sort of situation most people face in the workplace at some point. It doesn't matter whether you're male or female, single or married, the temptation to pursue an inappropriate relationship can be really difficult to deal with.

"The good thing is that you know what you don't want, so try to find a positive way to say 'no'. Think carefully about how you say it. Hopefully you will be able to let them down gently and maintain a good, professional relationship. Relating to your work colleagues in a caring way will speak volumes about your priorities in life."

In discussing the knowledge of God's ways, as we have done in this section, it is only appropriate that we touch briefly on the biography of one of the greatest business men ever used by the Lord. This is the case of a shoemaker turn an evangelist; indeed, one of the greatest evangelists of all time. He was Dwight L. Moody.

A brief biography of D.L. Moody, 1837 -1899

In discussing the biography of D. L. Moody, it is important to state clearly that no attempt will be made to discuss his crusades in details, we can only mention some aspects. The reason is that to write about his crusades will require a book of its own. In addition, we shall not discuss details of his life, rather we shall touch a bit on his early life, focus on some highlights of his life, his death and legacy.

Early Life

Dwight Lyman Moody, was born on February 5, 1837 in Northfield, MA. Dwight's father, Edwin, though an alcoholic, worked very hard as a farmer and stonemason to support his seven children but died when Dwight was only four years old. One month later, twins were born to the widow[54].

After father's death, his mother valiantly struggled to keep the home and children together, and rejected offers to part with some of them. Dwight and his siblings learned to share in the burdens and responsibilities of the household. Picking fruits, ploughing, working in the garden, and milking cows taught Moody many lessons that were to prove valuable in his career. In spite of these difficulties, he also learned early that hard work and responsibilities are a way of life, but that labour also has its rewards, including a strong physical constitution.

Some Highlights of his Life

1. Sunday School:

In the Fall of 1858, he started his own Sunday School in an abandoned freight car, then moved to an old vacant saloon on Michigan Street, Chicago. The school became so large that the former mayor gave him the hall over the city's North Market for his meetings, rent free. He later produced the largest Sunday School in Chicago, reaching some 1,500 weekly. Moody supervised, recruited, and did the janitor work early Sunday morning, cleaning out the debris from a Saturday night dance, to get ready for the afternoon Sunday School.

He abandoned his secular appointment in June, 1860 to focus all his time on his Sunday School work. On November 25, 1860, President-elect, Abraham Lincoln visited Moody's Sunday School.

2. Moody Church

In 1863, when only 26, he raised $20,000 to erect the Illinois Street Church with a seating capacity of 1,500 [55]. It began February 28, 1864 with twelve members. This was the official beginning of what is now known as Moody Church. He was the president of the Chicago Y.M.C.A. from 1866 to 1869 and participated in erecting the first Y.M.C.A. building in America, the Farwell Hall in 1867, seating 3,000. That year he also held his first revival campaign in Philadelphia.

In 1867, he visited the UK and Ireland with his wife. On this trip, while they sat in a public park in Dublin, Evangelist Henry Varley remarked, "The world has yet to see what God will do with and for, and through, and in, and by, the man who is fully consecrated to Him." John Knox allegedly originated this saying that was now to burn in Moody's soul (some historians put this Varley conversation in an 1872 trip). Moody met Henry Moorhouse also in Dublin and was promised a visit to Chicago.

3. Some Lessons from his preparation for his crusades

Three incidents reportedly prepared Moody for his world famous evangelistic crusades. First, in February, 1868, Moorhouse preached in Moody's pulpit in Chicago. For seven nights he preached from the text, John 3:16, counselling Moody privately, "Teach what the Bible says, not your own words, and show people how much God loves them."

A second incident was the meeting of Ira A. Sankey, while attending a Y.M.C.A. convention in Indianapolis in July of 1870. Moody was to speak at a 7 AM prayer meeting on a Sunday morning. Sankey was there. When Moody asked for a volunteer song, Sankey began to sing: "There is a Fountain Filled with Blood." Moody's direct approach was, "You will have to come to Chicago and help me. I've been looking for you for eight years!" Sankey left his post-office job in Pennsylvania and joined Moody in Chicago in early 1871. This underlines the power of praise in preaching the gospel.

A third incident was the Chicago fire and the ensuing filling of the Holy Spirit. On Sunday night, October 8, 1871, while preaching at Farwell Hall, which was now being used because of the increased crowds, Moody asked his congregation to evaluate their relationships to Christ and return next week to make their decisions for Him. That crowd never regathered. While Sankey was singing a closing song, the din of fire trucks and church bells scattered them forever for Chicago was on fire. The Y.M.C.A. building, church, and parsonage were all to be lost in the next 24 hours.

The church was reopened on December 24, 1871, and it was now called the North Side Tabernacle, located on Ontario and Wells St., close to the former building. There was no regular pastor at this church in its brief history, 1871-1876. While raising funds for the rebuilding of this church, he described a life changing experience he had upon locking himself in a room of a friend's house:... "one day, in the city of New York, Oh what a day! I cannot describe it. I seldom refer to it, it's almost too sacred an experience to name. Paul had an experience of which he never spoke for fourteen years. I can only say that God was revealed to me, and I had such an experience of His love that I had to ask Him to stay His hand..."

His death

In 1898 Moody was chairman of the evangelistic department of the Army and Navy Christian Commission of the Y.M.C.A. during the Spanish-American War. He started his last crusade in Kansas City in November, 1899. On November 16, he preached his last sermon on Excuses (Luke 14:16-24) and hundreds were won to Christ that night. He was very ill afterwards, the illness thought to be fatty degeneration of the heart. Arriving home in Northfield November 19 for rest, he climbed the stairs to his bedroom never to leave it again. He died about 7AM December 22, with a note of victory. He was reported to have said such things as the following. "I see earth receding; heaven is approaching (or opening). God is calling me. This is my triumph. This is my coronation day. It is glorious. God is calling and I must go. Mama, you have been a good wife...no pain... no valley...it's bliss." The funeral was on December 26 with C.I.

Scofield, local Congregational pastor in charge. Memorial services were held in many leading cities in America and Great Britain.

Some of his legacies

Moody left to the world several books, although he never wrote a book himself.

His Gospel sermons, Bible characters, devotional and doctrinal studies were all compiled from his spoken word, those after 1893 by A.P. Fitt. However he read every article and book before they were published. His innumerable converts were estimated by some as high as 1,000,000.

R.A. Torrey, one of his closest friends, writes his conclusions in his famous "Why God Used D.L. Moody"; he gives the following reasons: (1) fully surrendered, (2) man of prayer, (3) student of the Word of God, (4) humble man, (5) freedom from love of money, (6) consuming passion for the lost, (7) definite endument with power from on high. Perhaps the world HAS seen what one man totally consecrated to God can do.

15

Joseph Calling: An Interview with Gunnar Olson, Chairman and Founder of International Christian Chamber of Commerce (ICCC)

ॐ

T his is part of an interview of Gunnar Olson *by Os Hillman* November 22, 2006 [56][57]. It has been included here because it is seen as relevant to the message of this book.

Q: As you see Christians not only from the US but also internationally, could you describe the current state of the average Christian business person in various parts of the world?

A: The church generally has been focused on evangelism and saving souls. We have in many cases however had a rather shallow view of what it means to make disciples. In simple terms, we could say it this way: Christians have made Jesus as their Saviour, but they have not made Him as their Lord. However, it goes even deeper than that simple illustration. Jesus did everything by faith and in the power of the Holy Spirit. This means that everything we do must be a walk of faith. But I also see a growing yearning in many hearts to see God glorified in their lives.

Q: What is the challenge for a business person wanting to move into the walk of faith?

A: I have often compared a Christian business person to the nation of Israel when it was in the desert after having escaped from slavery in Egypt. In Egypt, they had been under their masters, fed by their masters and totally controlled. Finally they broke free. Perhaps we can liken this to salvation. In the past we were totally under the bondage of sin and the power of the prince of the kingdom of darkness. However, through the complete work of Jesus, we have broken free. However, many Christians are still like the people of Israel in the desert. Though they are free, in the desert they are still slaves in their heart. They are not willing to enter the Promised Land. They prefer the comfort and security of slavery to the insecurities of life following God in the pillar of smoke and the pillar of fire. Similarly, many of us find the security of the world system much more comfortable than the walk of faith. Our challenge also is to walk into our promised land. Therefore, through ICCC we have been calling the Christian business community to come out of Egypt, and the slave mentality, to enter into the full freedom of the sons of God. This is not just preaching. This is a very deep and powerful reality. As some of us have begun to move through these faith experiences, powerful testimonies have been raised up in various parts of the world. We are now seeing the people who have walked in this kind of freedom for several years and it is exciting!

Q: What does the "Promised Land" look like for a Christian business person?

A: My answer for business people is similar to that for the Israelites. For every believer, our Promised Land is a land flowing with "milk and honey." But some of the same challenges also apply. We often forget what happened when the Israelites first entered the Promised Land. When they crossed over the Jordan, the first thing that happened was a time of circumcision. This is a very serious thing and we often fail to think about it when we speak so freely about blessings. There is a time of dedication, shedding the former things, even some time of testing and pain and humbling ourselves, before we are ready to enter into the blessings. We often forget that the Israelites had to fight for the Promised Land. They did not just walk in and everything came to them. There were 39 wars before it came under their control. They needed to be obedient to take the whole Land. They could not compromise with the other people there. They also had to cast out idols in the Promised Land. There are a lot of messages out of this story that have important applications for Christians in business.

Q: What are the implications of entering the Promised Land?

A: It is a strange and wonderful thing with God that He gives man a free will. We are free to decide whether or not to enter the Promised Land. However, if we refuse to, we can be found like those Israelites that refused to enter the Promised Land in their day. They needed to be humbled and many even died in the desert. Many of us also go through times of testing and humbling in the desert. However the Bible tells us that God does this in order to do us good in the end. We need to keep the goodness of God and His love in front of us at all times. So we are not just talking about an optional role in which someone could get some extra "blessing". This is not an issue of being a better Christian or not. The Bible says that every-thing that is not of faith is sin. Therefore, when we think about a walk of faith, we really need to see that if our life is not a walk of faith, we are walking in sin. If God could begin to show more of us this reality, I believe it would cause a major shaking in the church and amongst Christian business people in particular. Of course there is a blessing to walking with God, and all the blessings will flow to someone who obeys God. This is wonderful! But equally, all of the curses of not obeying God also flow to those who do not take the steps into which God is calling us. It really is as simple as the expression that Jesus mentioned in His Sermon on the Mount: we can not serve God and Mammon.

Q: What do you see as the business person's calling?

A: Many of us need to see a broader picture of the role of business in the Kingdom of God. Sometimes we are focused too much on ourselves or the local scene. But God is calling out Josephs throughout the world who represent a "tribe", if you will, of people who are "providers". They are providers not just for themselves, but for others out of their abundance. Joseph was prepared through adversity and he was used to provide for a whole nation. He understood how to walk with God within a corrupt kingdom. I believe God is raising up business people to be providers in many ways during these last days. The primary thing we have to provide is Jesus. Business people have lived like the Israelites who had to "pump the water" out of the earth as a slave to water their crops. That is where many business people are still today. We have not understood our high calling. We are still viewing ourselves as slaves to doing business through striving and toil. We have been trained to believe we do not get more than what we can produce. The contrast to the Promised Land is that God said that it was a land of milk and honey and their crops were a result of the rain from heaven, not water pumped from the ground. "Not by might, nor by power, but by my spirit saith the Lord." When Israel had to exit out of Egypt, they also had to exit from a way of viewing themselves. Today too many business people are striving to make their businesses work. The promised land signifies "obedience and relationship". Blessings come as a result of obedience. Blessings do not necessarily mean financial, but certainly His provision is from obedience. We have noticed that the person who tries to take the shortcut never gets to the real promised land of spiritual blessing in and through their business. Why do you think the people got so upset when Jesus came into the temple and turned over the tables? It was business as usual as far as they were concerned. Their predecessors had taught them that selling in the temple was okay. They really did not understand who was the owner of the temple. When Jesus came into the temple He made them aware that things had to change. What they had learned from the past was no longer acceptable. He was changing their whole mindset about business in the kingdom.

Q: Are you seeing God dealing with Christians in the workplace about their commitment more so than ten years ago?

A: Oh, yes. It is much greater today. It is such a consistent pattern that we marvel at how often it is the same story among business people we meet. Especially among those who make a conscious commitment to serve Christ through their work. I believe the time is short and God is moving among believers in the workplace. We have noticed a very particular process (a type of death and resurrection) usually is experienced shortly after their commitment is made to Jesus for their work. The good news is that when we die with Christ we are also resurrected (Romans 6:4). We share with Him in that resurrection. Usually that person has greater success spiritually and professionally when they successfully go through this process. This is because God watches over their work lives and many circumstances begin to change that have nothing to do with what the person might do. It is a tough process. **The End.**

16

Role of Local Churches and Clergy in the Marketplace Ministry

ಠ

The statements contained in this section are mostly taken from views expressed by Doug Spada. He suggests that we need to consider the workplace as the major "9-5 window" for missions today. This is where real transformation can take place because the workplace is where authority is in the cities. He submits that we thought we could change cities through pastors and church leaders and prayer walks. However, church leaders do not have the authority in the cities. We need to equip and affirm the apostles, prophets, teachers, evangelists and pastors in the workplace. We need to think about building the Kingdom of God in the workplaces in our cities – prayer groups, bible studies, prayer breakfasts, outreach luncheons, etc. And we can help direct churches to other ministries who specifically are working with churches today as this new move of God is emerging. We need pastors to do what they are called to do – equip their people to be effective in the marketplace where they spend

60-70% of their waking hours – the workplace. In order to do this it has to be intentional, long term and foundational to the church.

Pastors must totally buy into it. Peter Wagner, President of Global Harvest Ministries and founder of the International Coalition of Apostles, sees this movement as one of the most important movements in the church since the protestant reformation. He believes that the only way we will see true city transformation in our world is to ignite the men and women in the workplace because this is their place of authority. Local church pastors cannot do this.

"We have been seeking to transform cities in our nation but cannot find one city that has actually been transformed spiritually, despite all the good things we have done. We have seen it overseas, but not in our own country," says Wagner [58]. Wagner believes the reason we have not seen transformation is because the gatekeepers and transformational agents are in the marketplace. "Pastors will not be the agents of change because they have no authority in the marketplace," says Wagner.

He continues by suggesting that there is a paradigm shift coming in the way we view church. We must realize there is a church in the marketplace today. The church in the marketplace is probably more representative of the church Jesus had in mind from the beginning. When a group forms in a corporation or marketplace, you often find more diversity in ethnicity and denominational background. It requires the people to find a common ground in order to have unity in their mission, which is often in the context of the unsaved, often harsh workplace environment. They are more likely to see their mission with a battlefield mentality than the local church because they are in the trenches and see the negative spiritual forces upfront and close.

Two Types of Churches in the Marketplace Context

Wagner says there are two types of churches today — the nuclear church and the extended church.

"The nuclear church is the local church that most of us are familiar with. However, there is an extended church where most of the people who are also part of the nuclear church spend their time. These two churches have two different rule books just like any culture has its own rule book. Those who operate in the nuclear and extended church understand both rule books. However, those church leaders in the nuclear church do not understand the rule book for the extended (workplace) church," says Wagner. Herein is a major problem in the movement as it relates to churches[58].

Ed Silvoso, president of Harvest Evangelism agrees. "The most common self-inflicted put-down is 'I am not a pastor — I am just a layperson. This is all part of a clever satanic scheme to neutralize apostles, prophets, evangelists, pastors and teachers along with the entire army of disciples, already positioned in the marketplace." Silvoso talks about this great division in the church in his book Anointed for Business that was released in 2002 and is currently one of the most popular books in the movement.

Christian researcher George Barna is predicting that the workplace movement is a major part of the future church. "Workplace ministry will be one of the core future innovations in church ministry"[59].

Role of Clergy to Support Marketplace Discipleship

Greg Ogden is the executive pastor of discipleship at Christ Church of Oakbrook, Illinois, and author of "The New Reformation: Returning the Ministry to the People of God". In his book he comments: "Robert Munger says the greatest single bottleneck to renewal is 'the hesitancy of clergy to trust the laity with significant responsibility. Too often our pastors seem to treat us as only fund-raisers (pastors don't want to be too closely associated with filthy lucre) or cooks or office equipment operations…when our hearts are crying out for meaningful ministry. This lack of entrusting to God's people both responsibility and authority for authentic ministry betrays the priestly view of the pastoral role. Pastors – perhaps unconsciously – have accepted the view that God's presence is borne by them to a higher degree, so by implication others cannot be full channels of God's activity. The pastor's distrust becomes an obstacle to equipping those who may be more gifted than they to carry out certain kinds of ministry. For how can the professional trust the untrained with people's lives? If you want it done right, you must do it yourself "[60].

Pastor Harry Heintz of the Brunswick Presbyterian Church in Troy, New York agrees with Ogden. In their church, they have abolished the term laity and avoid using any terminology that would elevate the offices of vocational pastor more than any member of their church. Heintz sees this elevation of clergy as one of the most damaging things churches do that prevent workplace believers from seeing themselves as priests in the marketplace and equal in their spiritual callings.

"There is a certain fear that comes over a pastor when you begin to talk about a workplace ministry," says Rich Marshall, author of God@Work and pastor for 35 years, now working full time in the workplace movement. "They fear that the marketplace believer is going to take over their church. They fear losing their tithe. They fear losing control." The interesting thing is that when pastors start equipping those in the workplace to fulfil their unique call, the exact opposite takes place. These people become your greatest asset. They bring others to your church. They actually give more money." Rich began ordaining people in his church to their call to the workplace to be on par with those he ordained for vocational ministry.

Training Required for the Laity: Marketplace Christians

There are signs of the movement beginning to penetrate this void of training. As we have already read about Doug Spada, who has begun the ministry called His Church at Work, which is a comprehensive training and equipping ministry designed exclusively for the local church. He has a passion to help pastors and local churches understand the workplace believer in their church and to help equip them to be ministers in their workplaces. He has created a professional website that serves churches, that is: http:// www.hischurchat-work.org, and provides tools and strategies for the local church to make this a priority. He has several major churches in the US that have contracted with him to help bring this into their churches.

Recognition of Church-based and not Marketplace Discipleship Programs Marketplace ministry is the road for 21st Century missions. It is a road once travelled with great success by the Church in its early history. It is the road the Apostle Paul exhorted the church to travel when he states that the purpose of the church professionals, that is: prophets, apostles, evangelists, pastors, and teachers, is to equip the saints to do the ministry rather than to just do the ministry themselves, Ephesians 4:11-16. However, some of the current failings of the church in this respect include the following:

1. It has reserved ministry to church based programs as it hardly sees secular work as a ministry. For example, marketplace Christians are rarely asked to share about their ministry in the marketplace at church meetings but they are encouraged to "make time" for church ministry in the evenings and on weekends. For example, a visiting missionary from "foreign mission fields" is often given time, probably much of the evening service time, to share with

the church their work since their last visit. The marketplace disciple is hardly ever given such time to share their experiences at their own mission field. The reason for such sharing is to enable the church to encourage and to support the missionary. Also, it enables the visiting missionary to highlight prayer points for the church. This happens in churches both in developed and developing nations. This activity of sharing reserved for the visiting missionary presupposes that the marketplace disciple has nothing to share or that their activities and ministries do not exist or are not significant enough to deserve such sharing.

2. The church professionals recruit marketplace Christians to be "plugged into" the church based ministry programs.

3. Those who are especially good at church based ministry are encouraged to leave their secular employment and join the church so they can minister "full time".

4. Thus most ministry done by the church is church-based as opposed to marketplace-based which makes it distant from the vast majority of people who live and work in the marketplace. This invariably limits the spread of the gospel because these people who are met daily at the workplace by the Christian at work will not be met by the pastor and other members of the clergy. Therefore, they will have to depend on the marketplace disciple to present the word of God to them. Besides, a lot of people who do not go to church could be won to the Lord probably only through their Christian workplace colleagues. This is

why the marketplace disciple needs all the encouragement, support, and prayers.

5. In order to appreciate the importance of marketplace-ministry, we must return to a Biblical world view that sees all of life as integrated and all believers called to minister in every sphere of society including the marketplace. This is one of the ways that the Lord will bring transformation into every area of society. Work has been *corrupted* but not *cursed* because of the fall. God values "secular" work, not just so that Christians can witness to unbelievers, but because, through transformed work, glory and honour will be brought to our nations. "Righteousness exalts a nation but sin is a reproach to any people" Proverbs 14:34.

Marketplace Sharing in a UK Church: It is not correct to tar every pastor or church leader with this brush of lack of interest in the ministries of marketplace disciples. For, the author was a member of a church in Hereford England where probably once a month on a Sunday morning, the pastor conducts an activity given the acronym "TTT" - This Time Tomorrow. He requests each of three selected members to tell the church about their secular jobs. These persons are encouraged to dress formally as they normally do at work. Each person discusses what their daily job entails, and also touches on any opportunities for witnessing for the Lord. Each concludes their account by highlighting any difficulties and prayer points. Immediately after this sharing, prayers are said for them, and points to add to our normal prayer topics are stressed. This practice could be commended to other churches because it gives room for sharing by the marketplace disciples.

17

Recognising the Priestly Calling to the Marketplace Discipleship

ç

I n this chapter we shall repeat a statement by Doug Spada on the marketplace ministry. We shall quote action steps by Os Hillman, and Core Values of WorkLife Ministry on marketplace discipleship as they contain very relevant information on marketplace discipleship. We shall give a short biography of a Christian banker highlighting his work in the marketplace and then characteristics of real-life churches in new Zealand involved in preparing their members for marketplace discipleship.

Doug Spada says: "I have a burden to help the local church pastor understand how to reach the workplace believer who is crying out to know how to impact his or her workplace for Christ. When we consider that the workplace is where the majority of people spend the majority of their time interacting with the majority of lost people, we realize what a ripe mission field the workplace represents. Pastors often don't know how to relate to the workplace believer.

And because I come out of the workplace, I can help the church understand the needs of the Christian in the workplace that is sitting in their church every week" [19].

Some Action Steps for the Local Church, Mobilize Men and Women to see their Work as a Calling [61].

These are actions a pastor and local church could take to mobilize men and women to see their work as a calling and ministry from God. These steps should help a local church become a workplace ministry-friendly church. Here are some ideas and strategies. These have been taken from the work of Os Hillman.

1. Establish a team of intercessors to pray for workplace believers, businesses, and pray for God to raise up a strategy of ministry to workplace believers in your church.
2. Present examples of workplace transformation to your body to inspire personal application in different types of workplace environments.
3. Preach sermons related to workplace applications. Form a team of workplace believers from different vocations to give input on the type of sermons that should be preached to address the felt needs of those in the workplace. In addition, teach a theology of work to young people so they do not have to relearn God's view of work.

4. Do a survey among those in the church on a Sunday or other day that asks this question:

How might our church help you apply your biblical faith in the context of your daily work life? Provide five ideas our church could do that would help you do this.

5. Start an on-going workplace ministry/outreach that mobilizes your entire congregation into the workplace. His Church at Work, now called WorkLife Incorporated, can launch a **WorkLife Support Center** online for your church. The contact information is available at their website: http://www.hischurchatwork.org

6. Preach a series of messages on the priesthood of all believers in the context of work. Preach on the five-fold ministry in Ephesians 4 and how these gifts and offices are in the workplace.

7. Remove formal titles of church staff that would tend to place them spiritually above members in the church but reinforce that each person's call is equal in the site of God. (This does not mean church leaders are not the spiritual leaders and shepherds).

Comment: This writer has observed varied behaviours of clergymen on issue of titles. The first time that he was in the UK, he was a bit taken aback to find that the pastors were called by their names and not with any titles attached. He therefore found it a bit awkward to call his pastor by his first name such as Derek, Philip, Antony, etc. He had to explain to some of them that he had been used to calling his pastor as "pastor" since it is the practice in his developing country. While some tolerated this habit out of consideration to him; telling him that he was free to call them by any name he found convenient, others rejected it. One of the pastors explained to him that we are all priests before the Lord, he happens to be called to be a pastor as his job. He asked him, how would you feel if "I decided to call you "engineer" or "scientist" instead of your name?" Following this strong and splendidly uncompromising stance, this writer has learnt to call his pastor by his name, even though sometimes, he still makes the mistake of calling him by the title and corrects himself when he realises the mistake.

8. Avoid addressing or favouring only those with influence. Equip and train the whole work force for ministry in the workplace. Be inclusive of the entire congregation including mothers, students, executives, construction workers and professionals. We often isolate the masses by this emphasis and our language.

9. Affirm workplace believers that their call is equal to vocational ministries.

10. Understand the problem that often separates workplace believers from church leaders.

11. Affirm workplace believers through church commissioning services focused on the church recognizing and confirming their calling (vocation) in a formal way.

12. There are hundreds of workplace ministries that can be a resource for your local church. These ministries can often provide helpful advice and equipping resources.

13. Provide discipleship opportunities for your people. Several workplace ministries offer online devotions. Os Hillman's *TGIF Today God Is First* email devotional is a free daily email that helps men and women apply biblical faith in their daily workplace. (www.marketplaceleaders.org) Marketplace-Network is another resource (www.marketplace-network.org), (hischurchatwork.org for churches).

14. Ed Silvoso offers an **Anointed for Business** conference that also provides excellent teaching on what it means to transform the workplace for Christ.

Os Hillman teaches a one-day workshop entitled, **Called to the Workplace** that is designed to equip your workplace believers to see their work as a ministry.

15. Begin a small group ministry in the workplace. **Priority Associates, Priority Insights, and Needles Eye Ministries** are three ministries that have excellent resources and tips on how to host a successful small group in the workplace.

16. Read the most important books on the movement and make them available through your church bookstore. See each workplace ministry's selection of products and books for examples.

17. Establish a SWAT (Spiritual Warfare Attack Team) team of intercessors from your church who are willing to go into businesses and pray for the leaders of those businesses. Their role is to go into different businesses to help discern issues in the business that may be hindering God's blessing upon the business.

18. Place a workplace emphasis on your missions or outreach giving budget in order to focus your church in this area. You can also support workplace ministries of your choice that equip men and women in the workplace such as ICWM which services the entire movement.

19. **Marketplace Network** specializes in equipping the professionals and career minded in your church. They also provide a *"How To Start A Marketplace Ministry in Your Church"* kit that can help you get a start with bible studies and other resources designed at this audience.

20. Begin to teach and equip your people to see their work as a ministry through preaching, teaching and equipping. (see www. HisChurchatWork.org for content on teaching, equipping and sermon messages). You may wish to download powerpoint presentations by Os Hillman and Rich Marshall that can be used in teaching and training. www.icwm.net and http://www.godisworking.com

21. Study successful church models that are operating based on these philosophies. (see His Church at Work & ICWM site for models of church based ministries).

22. Invite guest speakers on Sunday to address the faith and work issues to introduce them to the movement and their unique calling to their vocations.

23. If it can be arranged, once a week spend a few hours with one member in his place of work for a few hours. Get a feel for the struggles and opportunities his workplace provides.

24. Allow one or two people each week to stand up and share a brief testimony on how they experienced God's presence in their workplace that week.

Relevant Observations: The following observations are considered relevant for any group intending to implement some of these action steps:

1. A pastor has correctly observed, in my opinion, that any market group set up in a church should be under the control of the church and not independent of it.

2. A local church could implement what it considers helpful in achieving an effective marketplace ministry. It is not imperative that all the action steps have to be implemented. A church should weigh the implications of any steps that it wishes to implement.

The Work Life Core Values [62]

Please note that the WorkLife was formerly known as His Church at Work. These core values have been taken verbatim from their website.

Quote:

"We are passionate about our Core Values regarding the significance of WorkLife Discipleship and Outreach. They drive our direction and Worklife innovation:

1) Every follower of Christ is in "full-time" ministry. Every believer is a minister.

2) Our individual "calling" is principal to everything we do. We are first called to a personal relationship with Jesus Christ, then a fruitful ministry that flows from this relationship. Our work is one major focus of this calling and thus is ordained by God for His purposes.

3) The separation and division of a "sacred" calling from a "secular" calling is counterproductive and a non scriptural view of a person's role in the Church body.

4) God is a worker. God views work in the world as an act of worship to Him, and a crucial platform for reaching the world for Christ. Work was created by God and is a holy calling. **John 5:17**

5) Our global work platform is one of the largest mission fields in the world, and where Christians spend more than 50% of their waking hours and interact with the majority of their relationships.

6) The local church is called to equip and empower God's people to do the "work of ministry" through their *whole* life, including their work. **Ephesians 4:11-12**

7) The local church (gathered church) is God's institution for corporate ministry, and a believer's life at work (ministry) should be an *active and integral extension* (scattered church) of the local congregation's ministry and mission.

8) Our focus in equipping the body is inclusive. We are dedicated to helping all believer's who work. We define work inclusively to include all forms of work and all occupations."

Unquote

Chuck Ripka – A Christian Banker in the Marketplace [63]
Below is a short write-up taken from a publication in the New York Times with comments and narration by Os Hillman.

Quote: ""I'm Chuck Ripka," he said. I was encouraged to meet Chuck while I was in the Minneapolis area by one of my board members of the International Coalition of Workplace Ministries (ICWM). He had informed me about something special that was taking place in the Riverview Community Bank and the city of Elk

River. Pastors and marketplace leaders and civic leaders gather on a regular basis for prayer. The mayor of the city officially invited Jesus to be Lord over their city. However, this day I wanted to learn more about Chuck's story and his own personal journey. As Chuck began to tell me his story he used terms like "God said this to me" or "the Lord said he was going to do this or that." He was confident in his ability to hear God's voice. He recalls God saying to him on Oct 20. 1998 that He trusted Chuck and that He wanted Chuck to take Him out of the box he had Him (Jesus) in. According to Chuck, nothing has been the same since.

As director of the International Coalition of Workplace Ministries and Marketplace Leaders I hear lots of testimonies from those in the marketplace. So, I needed to know if Chuck was the real deal. Over the next year I got to know Chuck better by visiting the bank and his staff and speaking to more than 300 people a community luncheon in Elk River. What has taken place in Elk River will shock you.

Not Your Ordinary Bank

The bank just began in March of 2003. First year projections were $16 million in deposits but actual deposits in the first year came in at $52 million. Their original projection was to be at $50 million in five years. After 21 months deposits are now at $80 million. Chuck says, "One of the things the Lord told me was, 'Chuck, if you will be obedient to My Word, you will not have to worry about the bottom line.'"

Probably more important than the success of the bank is what has taken place spiritually. In the first 21 months Chuck has seen 80 personal decisions for Christ made inside the bank and almost the same number in physical healing. A video clip was developed by a Minneapolis company that portrays what is taking place in the bank and includes a personal testimony of one of its customers who was healed. Chuck's team trains their tellers to pray for customers as the opportunity presents itself. This is just a snapshot of what's happening at the bank.

This bank was designed to be a Kingdom bank. The founders of the bank wanted not only to run a bank with ethics, integrity and professionalism, but they also wanted it to be a place of ministry. They are succeeding so much that even secular and liberal media outlets are taking note."

Examples of Characteristics of Mission-oriented Churches

These churches are discussed in the references and appear to be in New Zealand.

Characteristics of a "Mission - oriented" local church [64][65]

- The daily lives of those in the church is the mission
- Sermons talk on market-place friendly language about being salt and light at work
- Bible characters are painted in all their humanity and daily living illustrations are from work-a-day world of the audience

- Church structure is simplified to free leaders to fulfil their callings
- Health is measured by the impact of the church's footprint in the community
- The church initiates training, relationships, and programs for members out in the marketplace
- Spiritual formation includes work-life issues of calling, serving, skill and character development in the work-force
- Training and mobilization includes facilitating spiritual entrepreneurship, and being Christ-like in the work-force, including use of range of Holy Spirit Gifts.
- Training and support for travelling to and from work.
- Celebrate as community success at work – testimonies abound and are enjoyed by all – to the Glory of God
- Stand strongly against unemployment.
- Share resources amongst the church community – so that no-one is in need.
- Know the members, meets their needs, supports them as necessary, and equips them – in an ever-changing environment

Features of a 'Mission-oriented" local church[66]

- Church members are coming to Sunday worship dressed in their workday clothes and bringing some objects from their workplaces with them to put on display.

- Digital photos of members in their work settings are being screened during a time of meditation and prayer, while a song about the value and meaning of work is played.

- One large church has 200 work-place groups that meet weekly, in addition to its mid-week home groups; a person is contracted to prepare studies specifically for these workplace groups.

- A pastor is being paid by his congregation to spend one day per month working alongside some of his parishioners in their workplaces [67].

- Church in Auckland – prays for people to find employment, when they have a job, church again prays for them and commissions them into their new job as "Christ-centred

- Checkout operators" [68].

18

Unity of Efforts for Effective Marketplace Discipleship and City Transformation

ৎ

The Lord prayed for believers to be one. He said: "I do not pray for these alone, but also for those who will believe in Me through their word; that they all may be one, as You, Father, are in Me, and I in You, that they also may be one in Us: that the world may believe that You sent Me," John 17: 20-21. The Lord Jesus Christ was praying for all believers, whether clergy or laity, to be united, to live and work as one. We should be one as the Father and Son are one. It is instructive that the unity of the Father and Son is such that they never work at cross purposes. The Lord said that the work He did was what He saw His Father do or as directed by His Father. The unity in the activities of the Father and Son should also be the unity of work for Christians who are followers of the Lord. It is the same unity that should characterise our activities as His people. United activities should lead to our services complementing one another in building an effective witness for the Lord.

United in the face of hostility to make our impact on society

As a church, confronted by sworn enemies, we should pray and work together as the early Church did, as reported in the Acts of the Apostles. Working together, not necessarily to plan how to defend ourselves against the enemies of the Gospel, but to organise how to go ahead with the Great Commission in spite of the opposition. The following suggestions should engender unity of actions between the clergy and the laity in marketplace discipleship:

1. The Church to commission marketplace disciples

It is estimated that by the year 2050, 80 percent of the world's population will live in cities whereas only 200 years ago most of the world lived in the countryside. A writer suggests that : "Today, frontier missions are done in the jungles of Borneo, but it is the urban jungle of Calcutta or Beijing where the harvest is really ripe. This is where there is a great opportunity for evangelism and for the discipling of nations. To rise to this challenge, marketplace missionaries must be equipped by the Church to integrate their faith and work. They must be empowered to think strategically and intentionally about how their marketplace activity can serve the purpose of God to disciple the nations. The Church must commission them to travel the road of marketplace activity to reach the nations and to teach them so that they may bring their glory and honour into the New Jerusalem" [19].

Geoff Bohleen, outreach pastor for Wooddale, a 5,000-member Wooddale Church in Eden Prairie, Minnesota, another church that has adopted Spada's process, says workplace ministry allows his church to reach out to the people that they would never reach otherwise. "There's no way our pastoral staff is going to get into all those offices - but our people are already there," he explains. "Our pastoral staff is limited in terms of the connections, the relationships and the friendships we can have with people who need Christ. However, we've got 'Wooddalers' all over the place." This underlines the necessity for the marketplace ministry.

2. Need for Marketplace Fellowship Groups

There are several graduate fellowship groups and Christian professional bodies around the world which we can use as examples to start local branches. Such national branches should provide us with rallying points from where we can engage in activities that could help prayerfully parry the shots fired at us by the enemies of the Lord. They should also help bring us together to plan how not only to respond to hostile developments but also plan how to build programmes for the dissemination of Gospel in contemporary societies. Let the Church arise at the crossroads of society, in the workplace, in the marketplace of the cities of the world.

3. Integration of Efforts between Marketplace and Pulpit Ministries

Since all believers are priests and there is a divine call to the pulpit ministry, therefore there should be a divine call to the marketplace ministry [69]. In line with our argument and reasoning, both the pulpit and marketplace ministers should work together, each playing its role, such as has been suggested in this book, in the service of the Lord and work for His glory.

The priesthood of believers has two dimensions, namely: the vertical and the horizontal. The focus of the pulpit ministry is primarily vertical whereas marketplace ministry is primarily horizontal. The two need to be integrated. To achieve this, it is necessary to connect pulpit ministers with marketplace ministers. An example of this is Paul working with Aquila and Priscilla to take the gospel to Ephesus, Acts chapters 18 and 19. Paul worked through the synagogue and the marketplace to win Asia [69].

4. Four "Keys" suggested for Transformation of cities [69]

- To change the city, the Marketplace must be changed.
- To change the Marketplace, Marketplace Ministers must be recognized.
- To recognize Marketplace Ministers, pulpit Ministers or pastors must partner with them.

- To channel the spiritual wealth resident in the synagogue (local congregation) to the heart of the city through the divine placement of those Marketplace Ministers.

As already featured in this book, Gunnar Olson has suggested that[53]: "Many of us need to see a broader picture of the role of business in the Kingdom of God. Sometimes we are focused too much on ourselves or the local scene. But God is calling out Josephs throughout the world who represent a "tribe", if you will, of people who are "providers". They are providers not just for themselves, but for others out of their abundance. Joseph was prepared through adversity and he was used to provide for a whole nation. He understood how to walk with God within a corrupt kingdom. I believe God is raising up business people to be providers in many ways during these last days. Many Christians working in the marketplace in developing countries especially, work in "corrupt kingdom" as Joseph did. May the Lord give us the vision and desire to live with the discipline and focus of Joseph to work for His glory even as Joseph did.

Healing of our Nations

The corruption in our nations in the developing world is such that we have become our own worst enemies. We are not able to help ourselves in spite of our abundant natural resources. When aid organisations and other external agencies, including developed countries, send funds and other resources to support us, we mismanage them even as we mismanage our own God-given resources. The result is that many of our people are suffering and starving in the midst of plenty. We blame our leaders, especially the politicians for our failings. To avoid corruption and other ills, many Christians in developing countries shun politics. The truth is that we are making politicians who take decisions the scape goat. Public servants, private sector workers, business entrepreneurs, traders, indeed everyone is involved. We really cannot exonerate anyone, we are all guilty.

Necessity to pray for the Healing of our Nations

It is considered relevant and indeed necessary to give some reasons why marketplace disciples should feel a responsibility to pray for the healing of their nations. They include the following:

1. The Lord is interested in nations: As we read the Bible we find that God is not interested in the death of a sinner. He wants to save anyone and everyone who will repent 2 Peter 3: 9. It is equally true that He is interested in nations. He called Abraham and promised to bless him. Make of him a great nation, and bless all the nations of the world through him, Genesis 12:1-3.

2. The Lord is grieved by the sins of nations: When Sodom and Gomorrah committed grievous sins continually, it grieved the Lord that He was going to destroy the cities because He could not find ten righteous persons in them, Genesis 18:32. In other words, He was concerned about the cities and would have saved them if He found the number of persons He wanted.

3. The Lord had in the past sent preachers to nations: The Lord sent Jonah to preach to Nineveh. Jonah was reluctant for his narrow patriotic reasons but the Lord compelled him to go. He described Nineveh as a great city and He was so concerned about its welfare that He wanted its citizens to repent so that the city could be saved, at least at that time.

The Lord sent prophets at different times to warn the people of Israel of the unpleasant and dire consequences that awaited them for their sins. The call was for their repentance. Kings and rulers were admonished and warned over their failures. They were guilty of not just living in disobedience to God but also of practising injustice and leading people away from God.

4. The Lord Jesus Christ rebuked those who were leading the nation astray: The Lord Jesus Christ brought the good news to individuals and to the people. He healed the sick, fed the hungry, and met the needs of suffering humanity. At the same time, He did not close His eyes to the sins of the Pharisees, Sadducee, the priests and all the leaders who were leading people astray, rather, He denounced their sins. He preached to Nicodemus, a member of the Sanhedrin, the Jewish ruling council. His parting command to His disciples was to preach the good news to everyone in all nations.

5. The disciples preached the good news to everyone and prayed for leaders: The disciples preached the good news to everyone both the governed and governors. They admonish that prayers should be said for those in authority and in government. The Lord is interested in our nations. We therefore have a responsibility to pray and work for the healing of our nations.

6. The Lord will use both the clergy and marketplace disciples for healing the nations: Corruption is the bane of our development. As we pray that we walk effectively with the Lord in obedience everyday for His honour and glory, we should also pray that the Lord will use us as instruments for the healing of our nations. The sins and corruption in our nations are so many and complex that we pray that the Lord will intervene to save us. We know that He will not use angels but humans; we therefore pray that He will find Christians who will prove faithful. Christians who will prove to be honest in our nations where dishonesty has become a culture. Christians who will be transparently clean when others are seeped in corruption. Christians who will swim against the tide of criminal activities indulged in by many in our nations in the guise of service to the nation.

Christ is the Hope of our Nations

From our experiences in the developing nations, we can make the following analysis to establish the importance of the contributions that marketplace disciples should make in the healing of our nations.

Failure of education alone: It is the case that education on its own has not been shown as able to help cure our national ills and crimes. For, as we go through our national news, we find that there are well educated persons, professors, medical doctors, architects, engineers, lawyers, politicians, business leaders, etc., who are meshed in the corruption and looting of our nations' wealth. It is extremely sad and disappointing that in spite of their eloquent speeches, many of them are worse than the less educated politicians, businessmen and women in the mismanagement of our national resources.

Inefficacy of proven operations management systems: Installing systems to achieve checks and balances and transparency in public processes and operations is useful but not an adequate solution. Our unpleasant experience has been that as we discuss projects to achieve such desirable results in their financial and operations management systems with public and private sector organisations who should use them to achieve desired fiscal and personal discipline in project management and economic development activities, we are surprised that some of their interest is dubious. Rather than study and discuss how to use the systems and tools effectively, some customers think and talk mostly about how to defeat, bypass and disable the systems. It is certainly worrying that tools and systems that have been used with good success in developed nations are easily dismissed as unsuitable for our national operations because the basic honesty of the individual user that is assumed in the operations of some of the systems cannot be guaranteed among our people.

People who will not conform: Our culture is so seeped in corruption that dubious practices have become the norm. It will require people who, out of personal convictions, are prepared to buck the trend to refuse to conform in order to do what is right. Some of these are those with the fear of God in them. Those who wish to obey and please God rather than man. These people will pass the Mammon Test.

19

Conclusion: Man in Christ is Man at His Best

ê

Earlier in this book, we made the point that the Lord brings the best out of the individual who believes in Him and walks with Him. We are a peculiar people, a people of the Lord, and should live such lives that reflect His holiness in our dealings in our communities. We gave examples of Joseph and Daniel, who even in foreign countries, lived God-fearing and excellent lives. No fault could be found in Daniel even when his colleagues conspired against him to find it; they could not find anything with which to incriminate him in his job. Daniel is a role model for the Christian disciple in the marketplace because he worked in the marketplace and honoured the Lord with his excellent performance.

Joseph also worked in the marketplace. In spite of his trials and tribulations in the early stages of his stay in Egypt, he remained faithful to the Lord. He did not abandon his faith as he faced one problem after the other, including being imprisoned unfairly. At

God's own time, he was released and moved to become the prime minister of Egypt. He did such a strategically essential job in the seven years of plenty followed by seven years of famine that the Egyptians were literally dependent on him for their daily food, their sustenance and survival.

Today, the marketplace disciples are the prophets that the Lord is sending to our nations. They are the Daniels and the Josephs of our time. We cannot afford to fail. The pastors and reverend ministers cannot reach most of the people in the cities and nations. It is only those who come to church that they can talk to. As we well know, most people do not go to church. The task is therefore that of the marketplace disciple who is God's prophet, priest, evangelist, preacher, and teacher in the marketplace.

The marketplace Christian should find spiritual home in their local church while realising that they will work and serve the Lord in their place of work. Each business person will function as a business person, evangelist, pastor, etc., all rolled into one at their place of work. The same should be true for the civil servant, politician, or professional. They should seek to collaborate with other Christians in their places of work to live and work for the Lord. They should aim at winning others in love to Him and at the same time live transparently ethical lives, and be effective at work even as Daniel was.

The clergy should realize they they have a responsibility to support other ministers who are working in the marketplace. Yes, they should see members of their congregation working at their places of work as ministers in the marketplace. They should be seen as people who have been ordained to live and witness for the Lord at the marketplace, in the front-line as it were. They should also work to support them and prayerfully help train them in the knowledge that they have the delicate balancing act and responsibility to reach individuals at their place of work even as they work at their professional challenges. These individuals cannot be reached by the clergy. The marketplace Christian is called to become role models, even as Daniel and Joseph were model, God-fearing marketplace professionals and were the very best among their colleagues. Yes, God makes the man in Christ; the man walking with Him as man at his best. He is a peculiar person, a royal priest, and a holy individual who walks in the light of God as graphically described in the next quotation: "But you are a chosen generation, a royal priesthood, a holy nation, His own special people, that you may proclaim the praises of Him who called you out of darkness into His marvellous light: who once were not a people, but are now the people of God: who had not obtained mercy, but now have obtained mercy" 1Peter 2: 9-10.

References

ॐ

1. Douglas Southall Freeman, Redeeming the Time, Christian Business Legends, by Rick Williams with Jared C. Crooks, pp.20-35.

2 Doug Sherman and William Hendricks, Your Work Matters To God, Colorado Springs: NavPress, 1987, p. 60.

3. "Are Some Jobs More Important Than Others?" Urbana.org December 27-31 2009, Intervarsity.org

4. "Entrepreneurialism That Can Transform the 9 to 5 Window" September 1, 2005,

5. "Loving Monday: Succeeding in Business Without Selling Your Soul", published in 1998 by InterVarsity Press.

6. Os Hillman, "Are We on the Verge of Another Reformation?" From Marketplace Leaders, 2004-2010

7. The Secular/Sacred Balancing Act , Otto J. Helweg , Interview published on 11 June 2004, Leadership U

8. R.G. LeTourneau, Moved by God to Move Men and Mountains, Christian Business Legends, pp.35-38, by Rick Williams with Jared C. Crooks

9. Hoyt and Alfred Buck, Christian Business Legends, pp.39-41, by Rick Williams with Jared C. Crooks

10. Buck Knives Incorporated from Answers.com

11. Dallas Willard, The Spirit of Discipline, pp. 214

12. The Dallas Willard Website: http://www.dwillard.org

13. Assigned to Design' by Andrew Patrick ACPA Newsletter, No 6 (Autumn 85)

14. Your Work IS Your Calling by Os Hillman November 22, 2006

15. BBC Historic Figures - William Wilberforce, 1750 -1833

16. Lesslie Newbigin, Our Task Today. An unpublished paper given to the fourth meeting of the diocesan council, Tirumangalam, India, December 18-20, 1951.
Cited in Michael Goheen, "The Missional Calling of Believers in the World:
Lesslie Newbigin's Contribution," at http://www.deepsight. org/articles/goheenb.htm.

17. Lesslie Newbigin, Truth to Tell: The Gospel as Public Truth (Grand Rapids, Mich.: Eerdmans, 1991), 49.

18. A Biographical Profile of Lesslie Newbigin by Brother Maynard, July 15th, 2008, http://www. subversiveinfluence. com/2008/2007

19. Jerry Higgins, Workplace Ministries: "A return to the original New Testament mission field ", Baptist Press, Feb 16, 2007.

20. TransformationForsyth.pdf, pp. 29

21. Changing the 80/20 Rule in the 9 to 5 Window, By Os Hillman

22. J. C. Penney Christian Business Legends, pp.8-12, by Rick Williams with Jared C. Crooks

23. Famous Missourians, The State Historical Society of Missouri, Website:

    http://shs.umsystem.edu/famousmissourians/entrepreneurs/penney

24. The 9 to 5 Window: How Faith Can Transform the Workplace., Os Hillman

25. Charisma magazine, May 2004 edition

26. Anointed for Business, Ed Silvoso, Regal Books, Gospel Light, Ventura, California 2002

27. About Ed Silvoso, From the Desk of Ed Solvoso, Website of Harvest Evangelism

28. Reference: Ruth Siemens – In His Presence, Intervarsity.org, January, 2006

29. BMS World Mission – Profile - Katrina and Martin Butterworth, bmsworldmission.org

30. Is there an eternal value in secular work? by Os Hillman, November 22, 2006

31. Living Our Faith at Work , by Dennis Peacocke, This article originally appeared in the July 2002 edition of Business Reform magazine.

32 Can a city be transformed for Jesus Christ? by Os Hillman, November 29, 2006

33. TransformationForsyth.pdf, pp.42

34. http://www.exampleofgrace.net/jeremiah-lanphier.php, http://riversidecemeteryjournal.com/page 6, Jeremiah Lanphier's invitation to prayer

35 Os Hillman: "Turning Disappointment into a Calling", San Antonio Christian Magazine by Os Hillman

36. The National Christian Foundation and Affiliates, 2009 http://www.nationalchristian.com/web/1/Doyle.asp

37. The Great Floridans 2000 Program, website: http://www.flheritage.com

38. W. C. Meloon, Christian Business Legends, pp. 48-51, by Rick Williams with Jared C. Crooks

39. Reformed Theological Seminary Foundation: The Architecture of Legacy: The Principled Giving of Walter Meloon, http://www.walterwalker.org

40. Terri Schneider, Communications & PR Coordinator, Correct Craft, Inc.

41. "Waves of Change, Central Florida's Correct Craft Inc., shows change is good from inside out", by Leigh Duncan, http://www.orlandonautiques.com

42. Henry Parsons Crowell, Christian Business Legend, pp. 11-19, by Rick Williams with Jared C. Crooks.

43. Larry Burkett, Christian Business Legend, pp. 32-34, by Rick Williams with Jared C. Crooks

44. Matthew Henry, from Arthur Wallis on pp.112, "In the Day of Thy Power".

45. Inventor George Washington Carver Biography http://www. ideafinder.com/history/inventors/carver.htm

46. John Woodbridge, More Than Conquerors (Chicago, Illinois: Moody Press, 1992), 312.

47. Legacy of George Washington Carver, University of Tuskegee website, http://www.tuskegee.edu/Global/story

48. Booker T. Washington, Christian Business Legends, pp. 28-31, by R. Williams with J. C. Crooks

49. Tyndale, Life Application Study Bible, pp.881

50. Kane, Herbert J. "J. Hudson Taylor 1832 - 1905 Founder of the China Inland Mission" in Mission Legacies, Gerald H. Anderson et. al. Eds. Maryknoll, New York, Orbis Books, 1994

51. Steer, Roger *J. Hudson Taylor - A Man in Christ*. Carlisle, Cumbria, UK., Paternoster Lifestyle, 2001

52. http://www.jesusloversincleveland.org/English/biographies/ taylor/hudsontaylor .htm

53. http://www.loveworklivelife.com

54. D. L. Moody, Christian Business Legends, pp. 40 -45, by Rick Williams with Jared C. Crooks

55. The Life and Ministry of Dwight Lyman Moody, by Ed Reese in the Christian Hall of Fame, Reese Publications, 7801 Embercrest Trail, Knoxville, TN 37938.

56. Featured Article, International Christian Chamber of Commerce (USA), website: http://www.icccusa.net

57. Joseph Calling: An Interview with Gunnar Olson, Chairman and Founder of International Christian Chamber of Commerce by Os Hillman November 22, 2006

58. The Church in the Workplace by C. Peter Wagner

59. George Barna, Boiling Point, Regal Publishing.

60. Prayer: God's Strategy for Success in the Marketplace by Os Hillman November 22, 2006

61. Twenty Six Action Steps for the Local Church By Os Hillman, Faith at Work, http://www.marketplaceleaders.org

62. Our WorkLife Core Values, taken from WorkLife Ministries, http://www.worklife.org

63. Workplace Movement, 31 October 2004: New York Times publishes article on faith and work: The New York Times Magazine, October 31, 2004, With God at Our Desks By Russell Shorto

64. Ed Silvoso, Marketplace Ministry, Sermon-Notes-28-Church-mission-in-the-workplace.pdf

65. John C Maxwell, Stephen R Graves, and Thomas G Addington; Life@work Marketplace success for People of Faith (Nashville,Tennessee –Nelson Business 2005)

66. Alister Mackenzie – Faith at work: Vocation, the Theology of Work and the Pastoral Implications – MTHeol Thesis, Otago University, 1998

67 Marc Gunther – "God and Business: the surprising quest for Spiritual Renewal in the American Workplace" Fortune July 9, 2001, 61

68. Pacific Gospel Mission, Ponsonby, Auckland – by permission of the Pastor

69. Ed Silvo – Harvest Evangelism 2003

Biography of the author

Dr. Okoro Chima Okereke

ₑ

O koro Chima Okereke, PhD, MBA. PMP, is generally called by his second name, Chima, and is a British Nigerian, and a project and business management consultant. He owns a registered company in Hereford, UK, Total Technology Consultants Limited, from where he works. He also owns the Nigerian subsidiary, Total Technology Consultants (Nigeria) Limited, in Port Harcourt, in the Niger Delta of Nigeria. He employs some consultants and staff who work in the latter company.

He is married to Dr. (Mrs.) Catherine Chima-Okereke, a Consultant Director in charge of Sexual Health Services, Hereford, in the UK National Health Services (NHS). They have five children, all grown up; three young man who work and live in the UK, and and two ladies who work and live in the US.

Chima and Catherine worship at Leominster Baptist Church in Herefordshire. They are quite active in the church, including the midweek house fellowship, and Chima takes part in the biweekly market-stall witnessing at the Leominster Corn Market.

Between 1996 and 2002, Chima served as a deacon at the Welwyn Evangelical Church, Hertfordshire, where his family worshipped. Before then, they were members of other churches in the UK cities where they lived. For example, between 1988 and 1993, they lived in Bradford, when Chima was doing his PhD and MBA degrees at the University of Bradford, they worshipped at St. Margaret's Church, Shipley Hills, Frizinghall, and later at the Sunbridge Road Mission. While at Bradford, Chima was the Chairman of the Africa Christian Fellowship, Bradford Branch.

In Nigeria, they are still members of the New Covenant Baptist Church, Port Harcourt. Chima was a Sunday School teacher when he was resident there and also served as a member of the Church Executive committee for two years. When they lived and worked in Warri and Sapele respectively, they worshipped at the Delta Steel Baptist Church Warri, First Baptist Church Warri, and Ebenezar Baptist Church Sapele, respectively. At various times, Chima served as the Sunday School Superintendent, Youths' President, and member of the Church Executive Committee.

He worked last in Warri as a Chief Engineer and Head of Department of Instrumentation, Control and Computing Systems at the Delta Steel Company Aladja before travelling to Bradford for his graduate studies. Prior to this, he worked in Shell Nigeria, Warri, and the National Electric Power Authority, Ogorode, Sapele. He was a pioneer staff of the Ogorode Power Station. He also had some thirteen months' training with the Electricity Supply Board of Ireland in Dublin.

He had his first degree in Electrical Engineering at the University of Lagos, Nigeria. At the university, he was a member of the Lagos Varsity Christian Union (LVCU) and at a point served as the CU Assistant Secretary. He became a Christian in 1970 at the Federal School of Science (FSS), Onikan, Lagos, at the end of the Nigerian Civil War. He was a member of the FSS Christian Union, and was also the Speaker of the FSS Students Union.

9 781619 044623